In this summer of fire comes this vitalizir...   ...e
archetypal dynamics impact the being t...
catastrophes in the relation to the (...   ...e
nonhuman, climate, the iconic gun, ...alism,
etc. brings soul-death inside the consu...   ...o treat it.
Susan Rowland, *PhD,* ...   *...Institute, author*
of ...   ...y Fire Murder *(2023)*

This challenging book aims to further the development of Jungian analysis
by paying careful attention to the importance of our present social, cultural,
and political realities. Our world has changed in a way that has radically
affected the psyche and soul of both patients and analysts. This change
has opened fundamental questions about analytic practice, the relationship
between our inner and outer realities, and how this change might alter the
nature of the analytic dyad. This work has brought together a diverse group
of authors whose engagement with today's challenges has made diverse
and creative contributions to a world truly on fire and to the heat and
development of Jungian psychology.
Stanton Marlan, *Ph.D., ABPP, FABP, Jungian analyst and*
author of C.G. Jung and the Alchemical Imagination

Laura Tuley and John White, editors (and contributors) have given us a
trenchant and definitive work; one which unequivocally acknowledges
the consulting room as a place where the political and personal can be
met—and possibly transformed. Each chapter tackles a compelling social
issue by incorporating established Jungian ideas and clinical practice with
a form of conscious 'activism' that pushes back on privileging the interior
life while eschewing messages of distress from our troubled, fragile world.
Whether taking on gun violence, racism, factory farming or environmental
crisis, these authors challenge us to heal and move past the old inside/
outside split in our discipline by allowing the overwhelming reality of
our world—with its inevitable effect on the psyches of both analyst and
analysand—to inform us body and soul.
Constance Romero, *M.ED., LPC, Senior Training*
and Supervising Analyst with the Inter-Regional Society
of Jungian Analysts and Co-Editor of the
'Clinical Commentaries' and 'Film & Culture' features,
The Journal of Analytical Psychology

Tuley and White have assembled a collection of essays that confront the reader with various forms of psychic assault emanating from collective trauma. Like fish who are unaware they live in the medium of water, they and their authors seek to remind us, to awaken us, to the co-created nature of inner experience and the outer world. They grab us by the lapel, shake us, and demand that we take notice of the toxicity of our medium and its devastating impact on us—and we on it. This book is a "le cri de Merlin" for collective realization and integration by actualizing a broader principle of individuation.

August J. Cwik, *Psy.D., Senior Training and Supervising Analyst with the Inter-Regional Society of Jungian Analysts and Former Co-Director of Training, C.G. Jung Institute of Chicago*

Timely and sorely needed, this collection invites analysts and therapists alike to look up and notice what is happening in our sociopolitical collective. Forcing our gaze away from our navels, we are reminded that we are inextricably linked to a larger environment where lives can be dramatically altered in a split second and where our engagement is essential. These voices offer hope for those exploring the depths that ecological restoration, social/political health, and inclusivity are part of our collective telos.

Jeanne A. Lacourt, *MS, LPC, NCC, Ph.D, Professor, American Indian Studies, St. Cloud State University, Minnesota, Jungian Analyst*

Tuley and White have put together a lively and thoughtful anthology that challenges conventional wisdom on the relationship between analysis (or treatment) and activism, and calls attention to the psychological toll taken (and the real world challenges posed) by urgent social, political and ecological problems, including environmental degradation, climate change and the impact of COVID and other zoonotic diseases; factory farming, animal rights and our broken relationship to the natural world; the evils of racism and colonialism; American gun culture and mass shootings; the ubiquity of human aggression; non-violence as therapeutic praxis. They point to the futility, indeed the perversity, of harnessing therapy to the goal of fostering adaptation to an insane society, adding to the small but growing literature that addresses these troubling social pathologies from a specifically Jungian perspective.

Daniel Burston, *Professor of Psychology, Duquesne University and author of* Psychoanalysis, Politics and the Postmodern University *and* Anti-Semitism and Analytical Psychology: Jung, Politics and Culture

Jungian Analysis in a World on Fire

This volume of essays, all authored by practicing Jungian psychoanalysts, examines and illuminates ways of working with individual analytic and therapeutic clients in the context of powerful and current collective forces, in the United States and beyond.

One of Carl Jung's central achievements was his clear recognition that the psyche is a locus not only of individual and personal experiences but also of social, collective, and even cosmological experiences. This important insight on Jung's part both opens broad vistas for psychoanalytic practice and poses potential challenges for the psychoanalytic practitioner attempting to understand and aid the individual client amidst the pressure of intense collective energies, especially amidst collective crises. Among the themes treated in this volume are principles of non-violence, environmental activism, feminism, ecological shifts due to the pandemic, the Chingada complex, mass shootings, industrial farming of animals, and death anxiety.

Jungian Analysis in a World on Fire will be of interest to Jungian, psychoanalytic, and depth-oriented analysts and therapists engaged in how best to work with individual clients in a time of social, political, and environmental crisis. It will also be valuable for scholars interested in understanding the impact of contemporary, collective traumas on individual psychology.

Laura Camille Tuley, PhD, is a Jungian psychoanalyst in private practice in Madison, Wisconsin. She is the coordinator and a faculty member of the New Orleans Jung Seminar of the IRSJA and Co-Editor of the 'Clinical Commentaries' and 'Film & Culture' features of The Journal of Analytical Psychology. Tuley has contributed to *Psychological Perspectives*, *Exploring Depth Psychology and the Female Self: Feminist Themes from Somewhere*, the *New Orleans Review*, *Mothering in the Third Wave*, *Art Papers*, *Hypatia*, and the *APA Newsletter on Feminism and Philosophy*.

John R. White, PhD, is a Jungian psychoanalyst and philosopher. He is the coordinator of the C G Jung Institute Analyst Training Program of Pittsburgh, president elect of the Pittsburgh Psychoanalytic Center, scholar-in-residence at the Silverman Phenomenology Center, Duquesne University, Pittsburgh, PA, USA, and author of *Adaptation and Psychotherapy: Langs and Analytical Psychology* (2023).

Jungian Analysis in a World on Fire

At the Nexus of Individual
and Collective Trauma

Edited by Laura Camille Tuley
and John R. White

Routledge
Taylor & Francis Group

LONDON AND NEW YORK

Designed cover image: Getty Images

First published 2024
by Routledge
4 Park Square, Milton Park, Abingdon, Oxon OX14 4RN

and by Routledge
605 Third Avenue, New York, NY 10158

Routledge is an imprint of the Taylor & Francis Group, an informa business

British Library Cataloguing-in-Publication Data
A catalogue record for this book is available from the British Library

ISBN: 978-1-032-18130-1 (hbk)
ISBN: 978-1-032-18129-5 (pbk)
ISBN: 978-1-003-25299-3 (ebk)

DOI: 10.4324/9781003252993

Typeset in Times New Roman
by Apex CoVantage, LLC

Contents

Contributors

Renée M. Cunningham, MFT, is in Private practice in Phoenix, Arizona, and has been a therapist for over 30 years. She is a Diplomate Jungian analyst and training analyst for the Inter-Regional Society of Jungian Analysts, and a member of the International Association for Analytical Psychology. Renée is an international speaker, educator, and author. She is the author of *Archetypal Nonviolence: Jung, King and Culture Through the Eyes of Selma*, Routledge, 2020, and a contributing writer to the book *Psychedelics and Individuation*, Chiron, 2023. You may contact Renée Cunningham at: www.reneecunningham.net

Jorge de la O, LMFT, is an analyst and president at the C.G. Jung Study Center of Southern California and a member of the IRSJA. Jorge is also a professor emeritus at Pacifica Graduate Institute. Jorge has published numerous articles, some of which include "The veterano in sandplay therapy," (*Sandplay Therapist of America Journal*, vol. 27, 2018); and "Los hijos de la chingada: The trauma of American internalized colonialism" (*Psychological Perspectives*, 2019). Jorge has presented nationally and internationally on cultural diversity and related Jungian topics. Jogre maintains a private in Ventura, California.

Stephen Foster, DIC., Ph.D., MA, LPC, NCPsyA, received his Diplomate Jungian Analyst's certificate from the IRSJA, where he is a Senior Training Analyst with the Memphis/Atlanta Seminar. He is an LPC, with a private analytic practice in Boulder, Colorado, where he works analytically with individuals, and with groups on business and environmental issues. Stephen has a scientific education (Ph.D. Organic Chemistry; Research Fellow, Harvard University) with a 35-years career as an environmental consultant for hazardous waste cleanup projects. He has lectured

on a wide range of Jungian topics. For more information, visit www.
boulderjungiananalyst.com

Ronnie Landau, MA, is a Certified Jungian Psychoanalyst and senior
training analyst and supervisor with the Inter-Regional Society of Jungian Analysts and the Philadelphia Association of Jungian Analysts. Her
private practice is in Philadelphia, Pennsylvania. She has taught throughout the U.S. and Zurich on a variety of topics. She is the author of the
article "Dreaming for the World: A Jungian Study of dreams during the
Covid- 19 pandemic" recently published in the Journal of Analytical
Psychology. Her interests are currently focused on the significant impact
of cultural trauma on the individual as well as the collective.

Dennis Merritt, LCSW, PhD, grew up on a small dairy farm in Wisconsin,
hence the title of his four volumes of The Dairy Farmer's Guide to the
Universe: Jung, Hermes, and Ecopsychology. He obtained a PhD from
Berkeley in insect pathology, microbial control of insect pests; an MA in
Humanistic Psychology from Sonoma State; and is a graduate of the C.
G. Jung Institute in Zurich. Dr. Merritt is in private practice as a Jungian
analyst and ecopsychologist in Milwaukee, WI. His two websites Jungi-
anEcopsychology.com and EcoJung.com have many articles on the environment, climate change, and cultural issues.

Randi Nathenson is a Jungian Analyst in private practice in Cleveland,
Ohio. Randi is a senior training analyst with the Inter-regional Society
of Jungian Analysts and serves on the Training Committee. Randi is a
member of the IAAP, the Pittsburgh Society of Jungian Analysts, and is
a former president of Jung Cleveland. Randi has lectured and written on
topics such as Mass Shootings, Kabbalah, Feminine Rage, and Racism.

Laura Camille Tuley, PhD, is a Jungian psychoanalyst in private practice
in Madison, Wisconsin. She is the coordinator and a faculty member
of the New Orleans Jung Seminar of the IRSJA and Co-Editor of the
'Clinical Commentaries' and 'Film & Culture' features of The Journal
of Analytical Psychology. Tuley has contributed to *Psychological Perspectives, Exploring Depth Psychology and the Female Self: Feminist
Themes from Somewhere*, the *New Orleans Review, Mothering in the
Third Wave, Art Papers, Hypatia,* and the *APA Newsletter on Feminism
and Philosophy*.

John R. White, PhD, is a philosopher and a Jungian psychoanalyst in private practice in Pittsburgh PA, USA. He is the coordinator of the C G Jung Institute Analyst Training Program of Pittsburgh, president elect of the Pittsburgh Psychoanalytic Center, scholar-in-residence at the Silverman Phenomenology Center, Duquesne University, Pittsburgh, and author of *Adaptation and Psychotherapy. Langs and Analytical Psychology* (2023).

Acknowledgements

We are thankful, first and foremost, to our partners, Chris and Kristy, who offered their emotional and editorial support throughout the process of laboring with this book. We are also grateful to our contributors, whose courage and vision have helped to fashion new pathways in the field of depth psychology.

Preface

The seeds of this volume were planted in the fall of 2019, during a meeting of the Interregional Society of Jungian Analysts, at which both John and I presented papers that could be characterized in this setting as "political" and pushing the boundaries of Jungian clinical practice and theory. At this meeting, we discussed with a shared sense of discontent the dearth of and resistance to such work in our society, and in the wider world of post-Jungian theory, even within the context of a meeting in which a conscious effort had been made to create space for presentations which spoke to the social, cultural, and political winds of the Zeitgeist. Initially, John contemplated organizing a "work group" to explore the relationship between the collective climate and the deeply interior expeditions we undertake, as analysts and analysands, within the containers of our analytic couplings. But soon we began to imagine a book that would address this seeming lacuna in the field. Our hope in this endeavor was not to disregard or reject classical Jungian psychology and the variegated fruit it has borne, as much as to expand and deepen its relevance for the clinicians—analysts and psychotherapists—of our time, who face challenges, battles, and pathologies that, in some ways, parallel the predominant diseases of Jung's era (after all, we, too, have suffered war, plague, political tyrannies, and social upheaval), but in other ways are markedly distinct (we have climate change, the "culture wars," and a technological revolution that is dramatically altering our conception of ourselves and relationship to our environment). Our intent, rather, reflects the spirit of Andrew Samuels' claim in *The Political Psyche* that

> the core of my project is to move toward an end of the isolation of the consulting room, though not toward the end of clinical analysis itself, and to work out the detail of a serious relationship between depth psychology and politics rather than huff and puff at the absence of such a relationship. (14)

Our intent, that is, is to dream Jung's initial dreams into the future, not as "Jungians" in the image of our founder, but as heirs to Jung's intellectual, psychological, and spiritual endowments with an eye to the intellectual, psychological, spiritual, and *ethical* demands of the soil in which we are rooted.

In the particularly tumultuous period since the 2016 American presidential election, I have pondered a couple of questions around the practice of analytic work. First, whether it really serves our patients to interpret their authentic, sensitive, and, paradoxically, normal and healthy expressions of grief, anxiety, and anger in response to the political and social climate from a conventionally analytic vantage point (one that focuses, at times exclusively, on the individual's inner world and navigation of the unconscious). I return, often, in my reflections to a passage from Jerome Bernstein's *Living in the Borderland: The Evolution of Consciousness and the Challenge of Healing Trauma* in which the analyst is confronted by a patient's adamant resistance to his interpretation of her grief around a cargo of cows she imagines are being taken to slaughter. The patient insists that she is responding to the experience of the animals themselves, for and with whom she is suffering. Rather than pathologize her refusal of an analytic position, Bernstein is moved by the patient's passionate rejection, which leads him, ultimately, to formulate his theory of "Borderland people" as individuals who possess and express a "psychic connection with nature" and are, in a sense, "charged" with the task of grieving our alienation from and destruction of the earth. This moment stands out to me both because I, too, have encountered such individuals in my practice and because I appreciate the author's recognition of the limits and shadows of our profession. Rather than press at or label her resistance, Bernstein accepts the patient's stance as both valid and meaningful, not just individually but for the larger sentient world. I, too, wonder, when patients bring me their outrage and sadness in reaction to a world in crisis, whether they are acting as vectors of a collective despair, and if their impulse to protest, regardless of its efficacy, might reflect the compensatory expression of psychic energy that seeks a restoration of spiritual and ecological balance.

My second question is about what it might mean for us, as clinicians, to express ourselves politically within and beyond the analytic container. Although the psychoanalytic notion that we should strive to be "blank slates" has been significantly reframed over the last century, there are still, for many arguably good reasons, explicit and implicit prohibitions around sharing too much of ourselves with our patients. But when, I wonder, are we called, even as analysts, to assume an ethical or "moral" position, whether that be in the consulting room or in more public forums and practices? After all, we are often permitted as clinicians to express our professional opinions vis-à-vis behavior or attitudes we deem "destructive" and unsustainable in our patients. Clearly, we subscribe to notions, however veiled, of "good" and "bad." So why, I wonder, should we draw a line when it comes to those political, social, and environmental issues of paramount importance to our collective health, like the threat contained in the rise of a dangerous political leader, in racism or in the degradation of the earth? I realize that this is complicated and controversial terrain, but feel called to pose my questions, nevertheless. As Jung wrote in 1947,

> as he has a responsibility towards his patients, [the doctor] cannot afford to withdraw to the peaceful island of undisturbed scientific work, but must constantly descend into the arena of the world events, in order to join in the battle of conflicting passions and opinions. (177)

Of course, Jung's reference to the doctor's necessary "descent into the arena of world events" could be interpreted variously, but what seems evident here is his evocation of the analyst's responsibility to participate in some way in the "tumult" of external affairs, where psyche also resides and asks to be noticed . . . that is to say, in politics. As Andrew Samuels remarks in *The Political Psyche*, "The Umwelt is both inside and outside" (4), by which he suggests that the boundary between the traditionally inward focus of psychoanalysis and the outer world of politics has no "permanent existence" or tangible truth. Jung goes on even more explicitly, in his introduction to *Civilization in Transition*, to confide that

> From time to time, I have felt obliged to step beyond the usual bounds of my profession. . . . This was hardly a far-fetched conclusion, for surely the most naïve laymen could not fail to see that many contemporary figures and events were positively asking for psychological elucidation. (178)

Here one might ask how we are to remain faithful stewards to the psyche's frequently idiosyncratic and amoral meanderings in the lives of our patients—as befits our role—while standing, "from time to time," on a sense of principle in the face of social, cultural, and political pathology, be that "standing" in the form of professional activism, personal commitments, or as muses to an urge to dissent. I would reiterate, simply, that the question is worth pondering, as there is no position of neutrality when it comes to matters of either psyche or state. Do we enable our patients to be "productive" citizens who function within the bounds of the given society, or are we midwives to the heterogeneity that fertilizes growth (theirs and ours), however disruptive or oppositional that might be?

In *'Two Souls Alas': Jung's Two Personalities and the Making of Analytical Psychology*, Mark Saban highlights the vital relation between inner and outer experience to the process of individuation, the pursuit of which resides at the heart of any truly Jungian analysis. He notes the inconsistency in Jung's own body of work, which at once privileges interiority and the psychic reality that unfolds in our engagement with the unconscious while also observing the indispensable role of the analytic dyad and, moreover, of a confrontation with "otherness" (that of both the analyst and world) as integral to individual and collective growth and adaptation. "[I]t is the very event of engaging with (conflicting with, even being wounded by) the other that constellates (and performs) the event of transformation" (2). We do not, in other words, individuate on islands of autonomous psychic experience or even within the sacred conspiracy of the consulting room, but rather, if we are lucky, via the messy commerce of inner "truth" and outer contingency that gives rise to both suffering and relationship. It is the necessity of such commerce, in our development as a species, let alone within our individual training societies and practices, that we must embrace if we are to address the demands of a rapidly changing and, in many respects, critically threatened world. As Saban warns,

> If Analytical Psychology, the psychology that Jung created, is to outlive him, if it is to remain alive and to continue to interact meaningfully with the culture, history and politics of the 21st century, then it must *itself* continue to individuate, and that means changing, transforming, reacting to, and engaging with the world around it. (3)

It is that individuation of the individual *with* the collective that John and I aim to further in creating this book.

Laura Camille Tuley

Introduction

John R. White

Psychoanalysis is, in many ways, a distinctly personal and individual undertaking, often focused on individual adaptive problems as well as internal struggles that are, and are experienced to be, totally unique—sometimes even feeling utterly inexpressible to anyone else. Yet one of Jung's great contributions to psychoanalytic practice is his recognition that the individual psyche or soul, though *ontologically* an individual, is *experientially* both individual and a participant in a greater whole—or in fact a number of such wholes. Jung sometimes calls these wholes "cultural dominants" and locates them, so to speak, in the "collective unconscious." We could add that among such psychic "wholes" are not only broad cultural dominants but also dominating ideals, complexes, and myths associated with smaller groups, such as one's own family, friend group, and profession, as well as other communities and collectives with which one identifies, consciously or unconsciously.

Seen in such terms, we can say that the individual psyche stands at the *nexus* of individual and collective experiences, a fact which poses its own set of problems when the collective in which one participates is undergoing severe duress. This is why we chose the title *Jungian Analysis in a World on Fire: At the Nexus of Individual and Collective Trauma*. Jung demonstrated that the psyche is a *sensorium* for both individual and collective experiences, while also claiming that what counts as collective is still realized and experienced only through the individual psyche. Thus, from an experiential and therefore clinical standpoint, the individual psyche experiences not only itself, not only its internal functioning, but also collective contents and processes, experienced consciously or unconsciously (or to some extent both), including collective traumas—a fact which cannot but affect an individual psychoanalytic process and raise any number of clinical questions.

DOI: 10.4324/9781003252993-1

Though it is commonplace among Jungians to speak of cultural dominants and collective forms of unconscious life, it is less common for Jungians to look at individual psychoanalysis insofar as it links to those cultural
dominants. It is, of course, a valid approach to collective phenomena to
analyze them as generalities since they are indeed general insofar as they
are experienced by many. However, in this volume, we are less interested in
focusing on these phenomena to the extent that they are collective than we
are in advancing the work of individual psychoanalysis and psychotherapy,
when it is clear that challenging and, in some cases, threatening collective
phenomena are, as it were, bearing down on a patient or analyst—that is
to say, when the world appears to be (or perhaps is) "on fire"—impacting
and potentially derailing the work of analytic therapy. Since the patient, not
to mention the analyst, stands at the nexus of individual experiences and
collective factors impacting the individual psyche, it is important to raise
questions around how to understand this relationship and wonder to some
extent whether we need to modify our clinical work accordingly.

With all this in mind, the following chapters treat of a diverse set of
themes, including environmental activism, the application of nonviolent
principles to analysis, the rise of the "dark feminine" in contemporary culture, the psychology and ethics of eating meat, the Chingada complex, the
problem of gun violence, the question of an ecological future, and death
anxiety as experienced during the recent pandemic. These themes are also
treated from somewhat diverse points of view. Some contributors, for example, treat their topic with a characteristically classical Jungian approach,
while others less so; some include a robust ethical component, while some
others do not. Yet amidst the various differences among these contributions,
what each one shares with the other is that each is an attempt to understand
this nexus, this point of intersection, between individual and collective psychic experiences, insofar as it may impact individual patients and analytic
processes.

In the first chapter, titled, "Our Climate Crisis: The need for an active
analyst when working with the Nature Archetype in Jungian Analysis," Stephen Foster suggests that adequately addressing the impact climate change
has on our patients requires that analysts become both trauma and climate
informed, that is, that we gain specific scientific knowledge on the role each
of these plays in our lives. The myriad of natural disasters associated with
the climate crisis evoke anxiety, anger, fear, and dissociation in analysands
and require a realistic knowledge of the nature of the crisis. Foster further

suggests that what he terms the "Nature archetype" provides a nexus for these issues in the psyche, developing the concept of an ego-Nature axis, echoing Edinger's idea of the ego-Self axis. By being aware of both the climate crisis and of the correlating trauma it produces, Foster maintains, the analyst is in position actively to bring environmentally relevant affects to consciousness, without necessarily becoming an activist or advocating for a particular position. The analyst thereby aids the development of unconscious psychic energy which allows the analysand to imagine a more mature and less destructive relationship with nature.

Chapter 2 is Renée Cunningham's contribution, "Archetypal Nonviolence and Activism in Analysis." For Cunningham, "Archetypal Nonviolence" is simultaneously a form of social and cultural activism and a philosophical and spiritual response to the violence from which it arises. Just as within the collective, nonviolence addresses the philosophical and metaphysical idea of equality and freedom for all, so the individual, each in their own unique way, undergoes an experience of activism in analysis, a response to the oppressive inner other separating them from the inner "beloved community" that can be conceived of as the Self. Nonviolent activism in analysis opens the path to this inner union. Cunningham explores the concept of archetypal nonviolence and its role in the American experience of democracy and the right to vote, from the Civil Rights Movement to the Black Lives Matter Movement and the 2020 presidential election, as well as the complex of racism, the cultural complex, and the forces of nonviolence that arise organically in response to the violent forces of the collective unconscious. The shadow side of nonviolence is developed in connection to classical psychoanalytic concepts such as *participation mystique*, the sadomasochism in hatred, and projective identification.

In the third chapter, Ronnie Landau takes up the symbolic and archetypal manifestation of what she terms the "dark feminine," illustrating the latter archetypally through a meditation on the mythology of Lilith. Though mythologies of the dark feminine and their concomitant experiences of rage are familiar in Jungian consulting rooms, we clinicians tend, so Landau suggests, to think of such psychic archetypal patterning as exclusive to women's individuation and transformation, something she believes limits not only our understanding of feminine and masculine principles but has powerful cultural and collective consequences. For Landau, patriarchy, and the corresponding repression of the feminine, impacts all gender identities. She suggests that the deconstructing of gender identities ever present in today's Zeitgeist may be symbolic of a necessary transformational process, arising from within the old patriarchal order, of what it means to be feminine and masculine. Though it is difficult to differentiate gender and culture from archetypal manifestations, Landau follows Demaris Wehr's idea in *Jung and Feminism* that society and the individual psyche are in a dialectical relationship with each other and develops her ideas on the basis of this same assumption, extending her meditation through personal and clinical examples.

In Chapter 4, "The View to a Kill: Conscious Cruelty and the Role of Ambivalence in Our Use and Abuse of Non-Human Animals," Laura Camille Tuley suggests, with Jung, that the more split off or unconscious we "civilized" men and women are from the destructive aspect of our psyches, the more violent and cruel we, as a collective, become. Consequently, since we are largely unconscious of and unrelated to the process of how the nonhuman animals that feed us are "harvested," we modern human animals in industrialized nations have lost an important aspect of our "humanity"— our connection to nature, in the indigenous sense, and the ambivalence necessary to mark and check our destruction of that which is not us, but which nonetheless supports us. Only by recognizing this damaging split and in recollecting the differences between sacrifice and slaughter can we regain our uniquely psychological role in the natural world. Tuley explores factory farming practices in the United States, the emotional and physical toll on both the individuals who labor in them and the public that ingests the products of their labor, and related collective traumas. Tuley suggests that our work as analysts in this situation is not only to heal but also to help us mourn the loss of the psychological limb we have severed in order to become "civilized": animal being.

In Chapter 5, "Cuauhtémoc and the Other: Confronting the Chingada Complex," Jorge de la O proposes that Jungian psychology has not yet sufficiently encountered the Other in such a way that it honors the unconscious of People of Color, especially regarding traumas associated with the history of European colonialism. In developing this point, de la O describes what he calls the "Chingada complex," a cultural complex derived from the unprocessed trauma of the Spanish Conquest of the Mexica. "Chingada" is derived from the verb "Chingar," which means "to be violated," the Spanish conquest often being termed *La Gran Chingada*. In working with Brown people, the analyst must acknowledge this complex, de la O suggests, which includes the unconscious memory of the Spanish conquest along with the individual and cultural traumas associated with it. As de la O puts it, "Jungians and others in depth psychology must not only concern themselves with the wounding of individuals, but with the wounding of the Latinx psyche and thus come to terms with the Chingada on the collective trauma of Brown people." To live the symbolic life, he suggests, it is not sufficient to honor traditions, but one must also come to grips with European colonialism and its shadow.

In Chapter 6, "Finding your Inner Gun: A Jungian Perspective on Mass Shootings and American Gun Culture," Randi Nathenson treats of what has become a recurrent tragedy in the United States, namely mass shootings. While mass shootings are the least common form of gun violence, the response to them tends to be strong and fraught with heavy emotion, fear, ridicule, and paranoia throughout the political spectrum. Nathenson examines American history, psychology, and culture as a way of reflecting on mass shootings, amplifying the symbolic meaning of the gun specific to American history and culture, for example, as a cultural and political symbol of power, patriotism, and freedom, while also using an archetypal-mythopoetic standpoint based on myths associated with the Greek god Ares, to explore this phenomenon further. Nathenson suggests that mass shootings point to an archetypal possession, the constellation of both a cultural and a personal gun complex, where shadow aspects of ourselves, including power, rage, and aggression, become enacted with destructive and fatal consequences. Nathenson includes two case vignettes to illustrate ways of exploring relevant shadow material, since it is often through the connection with our destructive parts that we can connect to our creative potential, harnessing the positive capacity of the "inner gun."

Dennis Merritt, in Chapter 7, "An Ecological Future Beyond the Pandemic," raises the issue of what the pandemic may tell us about our ecological future. What is missing in most environmental movements, according to Merritt, is a recognition of the intra-psychic world, particularly the personal and collective shadow that distorts human relationships and our connection with nature. For Merritt, Carl Jung addresses this issue with his archetypal interpretation of the Judeo-Christian religious tradition, one which explores the unhealthy association of the Devil with the body, sexuality and sensuality, the feminine, and nature and the consequent split in Self-image, symbolized by the dualism of God and the Devil. A spiritual ecology and a tolerance for different religious traditions can begin, Merritt suggests, with an appreciation of the phenomenology of the Self that Jung described, addressing inequalities at all levels, beginning with the "little people" in our dreams and extending to the tremendous imbalance in the human relationship with the natural world. The coming age, according to Merritt, will require working together as a species to address pathologies in the environment like climate change and the destruction of the rainforests and extend the sense of the interconnectedness of everything to our human systems and interactions.

In the final chapter, "The Jungian Analyst in Between Life and Death: Clinical Ethics in an Age of Pandemic," John White links key ideas on death anxiety from both psychoanalytic and philosophical traditions, as a way of interpreting psychological states and behaviors prevalent during the climax of the COVID-19 pandemic in the US. White begins by comparing ideas on death anxiety from Robert Langs and Carl Jung, as a way of highlighting two different approaches to death, one which sees death exclusively as the cessation of life (Langs) and the other which sees the teleology of life expressed in death (Jung). White then turns to some of the ancient Western philosophers who, like Jung, interpreted death as part of the teleology of life and draws from them the idea that the death about which one experiences anxiety is not only the death to the body but also what they understood to be the "death of the soul." The death of the soul, according to the ancient philosophers, is not its cessation, but rather a distinctly ethical phenomenon whereby the soul and its teleology are turned against itself through the development of vice (the opposite of virtue). White then suggests that many of the troubling psychological states and behaviors witnessed during the pandemic were in part due to anxiety over the death of the soul, a point which hints at a potential basis for a clinical ethics.

Our hope is that this work will engender greater interest in the points of intersection between the individual and collective psyche on the part of psychoanalysts and psychotherapists, and that these contributions will offer examples of how to think, formulate, and work with patients whose suffering includes working toward individuation while in a world on fire, spurring deeper consideration and ongoing research.

Chapter 1

Our Climate Crisis

The Need for an Active Analyst When Working with the Nature Archetype in Jungian Analysis

Stephen Foster

At the core of Jungian psychology is the recognition of and willingness to embrace the progressive energy in the psyche that furthers or encourages vision and a shift in consciousness. Similarly, an activist is someone who 'takes action' to authentically engage with what is presented to them in the moment, emphasizing the opportunity for a prospective imagination of alternative futures rather than remaining passive, observant, or inactive. An activist remains in relationship with the suffering inherent in the manifest content and supports the possible expression of action retrieved from personal and collective unconscious suffering and depression by working through rage, anxiety, grief, or despair. Further, an activist deepens our consciousness using a combination of active listening, education, and empowering one's relationship with the other so as to facilitate a change. In the case of environmental activism in Jungian analysis, the activist is stretching towards the recognition of the Nature archetype, a collection of archetypal structures that relate to our earliest origins in nature as identified in Foster (2011), that lives in the shadow of the personal and collective unconscious. The activist also calls feelings out of the shadow so the reflective psyche can begin to work on the process of change.

Reminiscent of Jung's notion of psychic change, Meares *et al.* state that within the progress of psychological work, how words are used is an important factor: "No element of the ecology can change unless the other elements also change. In order to bring about a change in the state of self, a change in relatedness is required" (2005, p. 676). When we model an activist stance, we are not caught in a narrow focus of the left brain, but the expanded imagination of the right brain (McGilchrist, 2009; Schore, 2019) where experienced images and their associated emotions are included in our analytic work. The activist is inherent in Jungian work through deconstructing

DOI: 10.4324/9781003252993-2

our structures of colonialist power dynamics in favor of a new consciousness that favors greater equality.

It was Searles (1972) who said, "The ecological crisis is the greatest threat mankind has ever faced (p. 361)."

> My hypothesis is that man is hampered in his meeting of this environmental crisis by a severe and pervasive apathy . . . based largely upon feelings and attitudes of which he is unconscious. The lack of analytic literature about this subject suggests to me that we analysts are in the grip of this common apathy. But a second factor, a special felt hazard in our profession, tends to inhibit us from making the special contributions we could make: we fear that an active concern with this present subject will evoke, from our colleagues, nothing more than a diagnostic interest as to whether we are suffering from psychotic depression or paranoid schizophrenia.
>
> (p. 361)

Searles concludes by saying:

> The greatest danger lies in the fact that the world is in such a state as to evoke our very earliest anxieties and at the same time to offer the delusional 'promise' . . . of assuaging these anxieties, effacing them, by fully externalizing and reifying our most primitive conflicts that produce those anxieties. In the pull upon us to become omnipotently free from human conflict, we are in danger of bringing about our extinction.
>
> (p. 373)

Where the environment is concerned, there is no longer doubt that "specific psychological defense mechanisms may be operating to prevent collective societal change. . . . Science is predicting a range of scenarios for the earth that are catastrophic for humanity" (Foster, 2011, pp. 18–19), yet another decade has passed, the climate crisis has increased. As a species we appear to be apathetic and lack the ability to prevent catastrophes and move ourselves forward.

Nature Consciousness and Shadow

Clearly, humanity is being challenged to develop a new consciousness; in fact, our survival depends on us developing a new consciousness—a "Nature-consciousness." The Nature archetype has been actively putting pressure on the human psyche to change our attitudes and forcing us to confront the errors we place in our personal and collective shadow. By contrast, our nature imagination values alternative ways of living, sustainability, solar energy, electric cars, and communities. According to Jung, shadow relates to issues we would prefer not to face or talk about, that is, "people, places, and things" we keep out of polite conversation. Where environmental issues are concerned, we disown our personal role in creating, contributing to, or failing to reverse environmental contamination and the climate crisis. We may deny our climate anxiety and minimize our climate-related depression. Putting our garbage cans on the street once a week is an obvious example. Shadow aspects of this activity are our failure to recycle and reduce waste at source, not knowing where the waste goes or how it is burned to create energy, not knowing how much carbon dioxide burning creates in the process, and not acting to change it. The activist in analysis draws out and, on occasion, confronts this shadow.

Most of us who grow up close to nature or who develop a love of the natural world are moved by its beauty and majesty. When we soften to the Nature archetype, we are called to recognize our own true nature—what exists around us also lives within us. Jung wrote: "Nature seemed to me full of wonders, and I wanted to steep myself in them. Every stone, every plant, every single thing seemed alive and indescribably marvelous" (Jung, 1961, p. 31). Jung held this attitude towards the unconscious.

Equally, when we see nature disregarded, abused, and brought into the era of the *Sixth Extinction* (Kolbert, 2014), it stirs not just strong reactions or emotions, but the inner activist may be constellated. When leading groups and teaching on the Nature archetype, individuals are spontaneously moved to tears or express outrage. A few examples of activists who have been moved towards action include the author of *Silent Spring*, Rachel Carson (1962, 2021), Julia Butterfly Hill (1999), Bill McKibben (2021) (author of *Enough*), and Greta Thunberg (2021). It was Searles (1972) who said, "the ecological crisis is the greatest threat mankind has ever faced" (p. 361).

A consistent theme they express is that rather than investing in long-term ethical and sustainable ways to live in relationship with the earth, we treat our natural world as an inanimate, unconscious rock, regarding the species found here as objects for our use and indiscriminate abuse; consequently, we have no respectful relationship with the earth. Even the pronouns we use when we refer to the earth reflect an attitude that needs to actively change to incorporate the multiplicity and non-binary 'nature' of the earth and its species. More relational theories have been proposed: the Gaia hypothesis suggests the earth may be an organism (Lovelock and Margulis, 1974); the deep ecology of Arne Næss (1989) advocates humanity as an equal with the natural world; this author recognizes the dumping of waste as a devaluing of the earth, which often occurs in communities that are also devalued and the least empowered to stop the dumping (Foster, 2011, 2012; Orange, 2017), and names the devaluation process as a colonialization of the earth. Our omnipotent attitude has brought humanity to a defining moment of emergency and uncertainty. Weintrobe (2021) describes it as omnipotent greed and narcissistic exceptionalism that promotes an unhealthy emotional entitlement that blinds humanity to the problems of the earth. Without including the earth as a legitimate citizen with rights and protections, it will continue to be abused and marginalized. The activist legitimizes nature, elevates its importance, and now screams for us to be in conscious relationship with it.

One of the challenges when talking about nature is to recognize more specifically the view held by some, that the earth is an inanimate object that has sentient beings on its surface, compared with the view that the earth has held sentient beings for millennia and that it, too, *is* sentient. The earth's sentient nature means that the whole earth is a lifeform beyond our comprehension, and the collection of species on the earth form a spiritual unit with diverse intelligence and consciousness. Either way, our relationship with the earth can form an I-Other relationship, based on concept of the I–Thou relationship (Buber, 1970) an I-Nature relationship which values mutuality, directness, presentness, and simple respect. In Jungian terms, this relationship mirrors the Ego-Self axis where the ego may be engaged with the larger, unknown, and unconscious archetype of the Self. A key part of Nature-consciousness is understanding that it represents an I–Thou relationship or an "I-Nature relationship" (Foster, 2011).

> We would treat nature as an earthly representation of Other, deserving respect in our everyday world, and we would relate to it seriously because of its I–Thou interaction. This requires dialoges with nature and with others about nature. With dialog we would become conscious of nature and our direct and indirect effects on her. This dialog would also bring the archetype closer to consciousness.
>
> (p. 19)

Scientists have known for years that the severity of the climate crisis will have an impact on humanity and the health of our earth. Because of their training, they may traditionally maintain their academic objectivity and emotional distance, leaving solutions and activism to others. Why have the most educated on this subject clung to scientific objectivity, rarely advocating for change when the evidence has been accumulating for years? In some cases, the scientists who have provided opinions have been overtly silenced, furthering skepticism, paranoia, and fear amongst those who are impacted, ultimately decreasing trust in scientists and science itself. As the full extent of the global warming emergency has now forced its way into our living rooms via images on television and social media, the Nature archetype has challenged and demanded that scientists share their knowledge, and many indeed have acted and even revealed the systematic suppression of data. Their participation in speaking out about the climate emergency or joining environmental action movements gives legitimacy to the call for a new Nature-consciousness. Simply stated, some scientists are assuming the role of the activist within their field (Wohl, 2016; Mann, 2021) and can no longer maintain their defenses nor their conviction to remain scientifically objective and passive. Jung's comment on conviction in psychology is directly applicable here:

> Conviction easily turns into self-defense and is seduced into rigidity, and this is inimical to life. The test of a firm conviction is its elasticity and flexibility; like every other exalted truth it thrives best on the admission of its errors.
>
> (Jung, CW-16, ¶180)

Despite the severe climate emergency issues that confront us on a daily basis, and its intersection with environmental contamination and destruction of our valuable natural resources, we fail to fully admit to our errors. The cleansing of our shadow regarding the I-Nature relationship remains essential, because

> Without profound purification, how far can social action actually extend? People involved in social action have a false self, too. They need to know the dynamics that are at work within them. Otherwise, social projects may fall apart, or they will suffer burnout.
>
> (Keating, 1999, p. 23)

APA and Psychological Passivity

In 2009, the American Psychological Association (APA) chose the path of objectivity when they issued their report, *Psychology and Global Climate Change: Addressing a Multi-faceted Phenomenon and Set of Challenges* (APA, 2009a), which recognized the problem and called for investigations into the psychology of climate change; however, the policy statement was emotionally passive. It fell short of activism in "Lobby government and other funding agencies to support psychological research" (APA, 2009b) in favor of educating the psychologist on how to talk with analysands about the climate crisis, refraining from taking an activist position to validate its reality (APA, 2011). Once again, the psychologist as scientist could study the facts while holding a comfortable distance. Then in 2017 the APA updated its position with more pressing language: "Climate change is recognized as one of the top threats to global health in the 21st century. Mental Health impacts of climate change are significant sources of stress for individuals and communities" (APA, 2017).

When re-evaluating the climate crisis, (APA, 2019), the APA's online document notes, "Acute events related to climate change, such as damaging storms and droughts, are associated with anxiety, depression, trauma and post-traumatic stress disorder." The document cites Christine Manning, an assistant professor of environmental studies at Macalester College in St. Paul, Minnesota, who says, "One of the most important things I do is to empower the college students I work with to take action out in the world and raise their voices for what they believe in." The APA has not yet crossed this Rubicon.

From One-Person to Two-Person Analysis

Andrew Samuels speaks to the issue of maintaining 'scientific objectivity' when confronting controversial issues in analysis,

> Many of us seek to fully meet such material, in a responsible and relational manner. However, we still experience the psychoanalytic dead hand, the penumbra of criticism that this Weltanschauung is nonanalytical and that the analyst will simply foist his or her political views on the patient.
>
> (Samuels, 2017, p. 679)

This is not how the activist within analysis works in these situations.

One-person psychoanalysis might be considered the psychological parallel to the scientific method, where the therapist assumes the position of detached objectivity and neutrality as an empathic observer of the patient's process. However, increasingly we are aware that this stance cannot always be maintained in analysis (Maroda, 1991; Barsness, 2018), and, with environmental and climate issues impacting people's lives, there are contemporary questions and challenges for the analyst regarding the ethics of maintaining impartiality (Orange, 2017).

The Analytic Third

In 1946, Jung described the intermingling of human psyches with his well-known diagram of the interaction between the analytic couple and their conscious and unconscious psyches (Figure 1.1). "The pattern of relationship is simple enough, but, when it comes to detailed description in any given case, it is extremely difficult to make out from which angle the relationship is being described and what aspect we are describing" (CW-16, ¶422).

Jung says:

The shared analytic space, or what Jung named the third thing (CW-16, ¶474; Cwik, 2011), is now commonly referred to as the analytic third, where the intermingled contents from the analyst's unconscious (in this case, my scientist) with the analysand's conscious psyche (in their case an emotional expression about the environment, concern or fear of environmental intrusion, safety, emergency, or crisis). These two aspects join together and press for a discussion of thoughts and affects such as survival, fear, anxiety, and grief associated with environmental issues (Panksepp, 2012a). With a global economy, the complexity of contributions to the climate crisis have

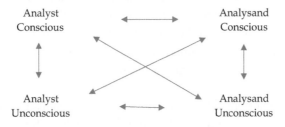

Figure 1.1 Adapted from CW-16, ¶422

become more difficult to untangle. We all remember seeing the satellite pictures of air quality in various countries during COVID-19, when the world stood still, and industry had stopped. The air was clear, heat and toxic gases were gone. Cities that had once had low visibility now had blue skies. Spontaneously, many analysands would comment on these pictures as if we all agreed a change was possible. For a moment there arose from this global 'experiment' a hope that things might change; the activist imagination proposed that consciousness might shift and those in power might be inspired.

Over the past decade, I have watched and listened as many of my younger analysands express how anxious they are in daily life—they have trouble sleeping, they seem to perseverate on things that feel out of their control, and have trouble focusing. I refer to this as eco-anxiety (Foster, 220). While this is not an unusual developmental condition for younger generations, the climate crisis, pollution, the degraded state of nature, and their passion about how "the older generation" has created the problem and failed to act to change it when they knew there was an issue are prominent emotional themes. They are distracted by the continued lack of political interest. Many send emails to politicians complaining or urging action, hoping this will assuage their fears. Others wish they could have an impact but express an utter sense of futility, feeling stuck, and overpowered. Mothers may learn of the polychlorinated biphenyl compounds (PCBs) being released from lighting in their child's old school building, or they read of the heavy metals in toys imported from countries that dump cadmium and lead onto the U.S. market that has few restrictions on foreign imports. Others express anxiety about high levels of lead in domestic drinking water. Indeed, the problems are prolific and ubiquitous, and the challenges are complicated and relentless, so prolific they simply freeze and fall into despair. Daily they contend with feelings of futility, and when the subjective experience becomes too much, they push aside their concerns by changing the subject.

So how do we work with these emerging issues in analysis? In his chapter, *Analysis and Activism*, Jungian analyst Samuel Kimbles (2016) notes that analysis and social activism, or in our case environmental activism,

> brings together opposites in the way we typically conceive of our analytic field. There are obvious issues around the analytic frame of neutrality, the use of internal constructs and the transference/countertransference with their emphasis on the dyadic, witnessing vs. detachment, privileged,

apartness vs. active participation or . . . how therapeutic neutrality is to psychic reality as witnessing is to the recovery of social reality.

(p. 166)

Kimbles speaks of the 'crossroads' that we face when these two opposing issues meet, and the analytic couple confronts the analytic third or 'inter-subjective space' that can lead to challenging moments that may progress to some type of therapeutic change. Kimbles says that working with these tensions not only creates a new-found space but also "releases the potential for humanizing the contact around differences, and for processing our mutual messiness when cultural complexes are activated and society enters the treatment room, filling the space with the hope for social change" (p. 166).

Samuels (2014) also discusses the effect of activism on transference-countertransference and the analytic relationship, exploring how the discussion of topics such as politics can be paradoxical, suggesting that if we avoid the actual topic, we may be avoiding content that is relevant to treatment. He notes:

When I first began to advocate that the therapist pick up on political aspects of the client's material, I was told that I might be depriving the client of the chance to talk about her mother if I kept her references to Mrs. Thatcher on the level of Mrs. Thatcher. I replied that I was worried about the opposite: that a client who needed to talk about Mrs. Thatcher would be definitely, albeit indirectly, discouraged from so doing, because talking about mother is what you do in therapy. In principle, any political theme can be taken under the umbrella of the therapy relationship.

(Samuels, 2014, p. 646)

Referring back to work by Jacobi (1965) and Edinger (1972), Mitchell (2020) draws attention to *The Jungian Dilemma* and highlights the ethical crossroads that resurfaces when working with the activist in mind. The analyst chooses to turn away from the authoritative ancestorial psychoanalytic voices of the one-person academy, to take a stand in the moment to trust and honor the topics that arrive in the consulting room. Perhaps the analysand's reality is not just avoidance, defense, or symbolically laden images with underlying parental messages but are serious reflections that reveal the activist in the client, and the progressive and prospective energy in the room, that holds the desire to be in an I-Nature relationship. I recognize that in my analytic relationships I am both conscious and unconscious, meaning that my cultural history as well as my professional selves are all sitting side by side in the room. The complicated layers and multiplicity within the psyche also suggest Jung's earliest views on the chemical reactions within the therapeutic interactions that cannot be colonized or denied but need to become conscious. We all have internal areas of diverse experience, training, and, in my case, scientific knowledge. I have visited and worked on some of this country's worst polluted sites and know directly what environmental contamination is and what it can do to the human condition, the human psyche, the communities that are impacted, and, most importantly, the environment or nature, all of which creates this analyst dilemma. The process of witnessing environmental anxiety, distress, and trauma firsthand, in its natural setting, is powerful for those who live there, as they feel seen, and for the witness, who can see and feel the energy associated with the experience. This is open to us all. In the western US, one can simply visit a burn scar, a mining town, or drought-stricken area.

While not discussed, many of my analysands know of my professional experience. Unconsciously, they sense my particular knowledge of and care for nature; these contents live within the shared field. On occasion, whether brought about by fire, oil spills, or explosion at a chemical plant, they will wonder aloud about this chemical or that, about air quality in their home, or about chemicals in the water they are drinking. They may pointedly ask for information, for my feelings or thoughts, or my 'expert' opinion on whatever is happening around us. I am reminded of when analysands asked during the height of the pandemic if I was doing okay—the question being not one to defend against and analyze, but one that was truly a healthy human concern that deserved an honest answer, that was then gradually unpacked in various ways that pertained to the therapeutic work. Samuels (2017) notes: "I believe we continue to struggle to find ethical ways of working directly, as opposed to making symbolic interpretations, with political, social, and cultural material as it arises in the clinical encounter" (p. 679).

Environmental contamination and destruction fall into all three of the earlier categories (political, social, and cultural), as the clinical example shows. While Samuels recommends that we continue to support our ethical and clinical boundaries in our profession, and in most times hold a space of neutrality, he is unconvinced that, when issues from the collective enter the consulting room, neutrality is always the best response (Samuels, p. 680).

However, I would go further where environmental issues are concerned because as an analysand becomes aware of the tension between the personal and the collective, such as the dilemmas of the individual's relationship with nature, or the environment they live in, there are opportunities for us to pose urgent questions that expand the field between us, nourishing and enlivening the activist. Samuels (2017) presents the use of nature images in this way:

> What, the client and I asked together, is the role of pollution in the soul, or even in the world? What is the role of pollution in the achievement of psychological depth? Can the soul remain deep and clear while there is pollution in the world, in one's home waters? Did the lake, with intimations of mystery and isolation, clash with the popular, extroverted tourism of the Adriatic?
>
> (p. 679)

Samuels suggests the relationship with the analysand can become animated, brought alive, infused with energy as if it were a mother or father complex. Yet, in this time of the climate emergency, these images are not just personal psychological derivatives of parental complexes; I would argue they are also derivatives of the Nature archetype that need active tending, given full attention, in-depth mutual respect with the notion of cultivating the I-Nature relationship.

What does this mean in our consulting room? In addition to political, social, and cultural material, when encountering the Nature archetype, we are also working with layers of affect such as anxiety, fear, dread, insecurity, a sense of overwhelm, and lack of control that reflect the unconscious aspects of one's community and the collective psyche at large. An obvious example might be when the analysand brings in environmental content related to a wildfire. We can certainly consider together what it might mean as an inner landscape on fire, the four fires of alchemy, or suffering from an inner scorched earth. We must address the fear of fires that threaten our survival and safety. The western US (Colorado, Wyoming, Montana, Oregon, and California) have been dealing with significant fire issues in recent years that have led to what some call a 'fire season.' We may even have friends and family who have lost everything they owned and escaped from fires with only the clothes they were wearing, barely escaping with their lives. If we focus on symbolic or metaphorical issues, we cause greater distress that may reinforce dissociation and compartmentalization. Although our own survival system becomes activated, we must avoid trying to fix or find symbolic meaning and instead remain close to the analysand's subjective experiences around current events that need metabolizing, which then opens the space for the relationship to the activist and the Nature archetype starts to come alive.

Is pursuing subjective experience over symbolic content really an environmental activist moment? A more important question is are we willing to entertain environmental issues under a subjective lens? Can we trust that the introduction of ecological content from the client is serious content? Are we actively listening, or are there times when their questions and concerns stimulate our own anxiety, our fear of despair or death, and do we dissociate, divide ourselves in two, and avoid the content because of our own dread or guilt? These few rhetorical questions keep us present to our current dilemmas as analysts working in times of climate emergency and environmental degradation.

It was impossible to ignore a local fire burning 6000 acres per hour nearby, but within the analytic frame, I noticed that some people slid into what was a familiar rhythm, almost manically searching for comfort by focusing on personal dreamwork and the symbolic with a need to escape the outer reality. So what about the analysand who does not acknowledge the fire or register a connection with their immediate surroundings, such as the strange color of the sky due to heavy smoke? Are they driven by narcissistic defenses, or is this also a symptom of climate anxiety? As analysts, we may feel the pressure of the dilemma on how best to proceed. In some moments, we may choose to retreat emotionally because of our own existential dread and anxiety regarding climate issues, such as a flood or fire, that we cannot stop. We may ourselves retreat to our perspective of professional responsibility to maintain neutrality. At what point do we move and become active? And can we actually influence a psyche that is seeking protection through primitive means? We are more likely to relieve tension and anxiety when we acknowledge the obvious, yet where and when is it that consciousness around the Nature archetype deserves to be acknowledged, animated by the activist in the room? The earth is expressing itself loud and clear, and for how much longer do we remain "still faced," as if everything is normal?

The pandemic brought an immediate way to talk about the activist and the Nature archetype. Because the coronavirus brought several complicated and unusual scientific issues, the analyst may have initially lacked knowledge or scientific language to respond to questions and concerns that have a biological or technical basis. As analysts, our own human anxiety, fears, and uncertainties about the prevailing circumstances may have stimulated avoidant detours into the symbolic aspect of the emotional content and unconsciously communicated that the topic was out of bounds. We quickly realize that, while unusual, it was helpful to acknowledge the rare environmental circumstances and the anxiety that was generated, even if the client does not. What I have noticed is a sigh of relief when I gently shine a light on the difficult realities within nature and we consider them together. This healthy modeling encourages moving towards a relationship with what is most worrisome, engaging with the discomfort, particularly when the environmental events are out of our control. By seriously exploring nature and environmental challenges, we not only invite the analysand to consider the environment we live in and are forced to adapt to as part of our individuation process, but elevate nature as something that is given the time and space to be honored and valued and psychologically vivified, rather than rejected, minimized, and colonized as separate or other. Finally, when we consider the plight of nature, we make room for our own *true nature* to exist more fully within analysis, recognizing what Jung often referred to as our own inner nature. In other words, the internal and external worlds are connected through an authentic moment of shared presence, respect, recognition. Through the retrieval of deep and penetrating emotions associated with nature, that have been disavowed, we bring the analysand's most inner experiences with nature into the present.

Personal Experience

When I reflect on my environmental career, I have memories of being impacted to a point of overwhelm by the magnitude of feelings generated by the significance of environmental contamination. My original training as a scientist was at Imperial College, in London, in organic chemistry. I came to London from the country, raised in a family that worked on a hop farm, within a family that encouraged education. When I moved to the U.S., I disappointed my 'Fellow of the Royal Society Professor' by rejecting the expected path of going into organic research. Instead, I chose an environmental toxicology program in Madison, Wisconsin, an agricultural land-grant school, where I did postdoctoral biochemistry research, that again diverged into cancer research at the Harvard School of Public Health and included training at the Harvard School of Law in conflict resolution using a tool called "risk assessment." In the late 1980s, risk assessment still offered a powerful mandated structure for cleanup, and I learned to manage large, complex contamination projects. While at work, I had little awareness that my unconscious was absorbing the anxiety and grief associated with the contamination and cleanup of sites predominately located in poor communities, or beautiful, majestic settings where the land was dominated by caste structures (Wilkerson, 2020). Having traversed the class system in the U.K., I was well aware of how the environmental cleanup campaign intersected with social justice issues and the indiscriminate use of indigenous lands for pipeline corridors, inner city neighborhoods for some of the dirtiest industries, and disadvantaged communities for dumping our waste.

On reflection, my inner country boy from East Sussex was growing more and more depressed; the indigenous part of my psyche was becoming more colonized by the left-brain narrow focus of my work, and the world of science forced me to abandon the imagination of my right-brain subjective knowing and its relationship with nature. Perhaps McGilchrist (2009) had seen what I could not. Allan Schore (2019) summarizes it this way:

> The left hemisphere is continuing to take precedence over the right hemisphere in the current state of world affairs, with potentially disastrous consequences. At this moment in time the present current leadership reflects this imbalance, reflecting increased left hemisphere power motivation at the expense of our disregard for right-hemisphere communal welfare. The right-hemisphere unconscious mind of a leader at the apex of power deeply influences the culture's collective unconscious and may be an important source of current political, cultural and psychological insecurity.
>
> (p. 210)

Unconsciously, I had formed a right-brain emotional relationship with the cleanup sites I was working on. In a state of deep melancholy and suffering, while working in Chicago, I entered Jungian analysis and immediately engaged with the shadow associated with this split in my psyche that we might imagine as Winnicott's false and true self, or the left and right hemispheric states of mind. I had finally found a place where, as my analyst sat with me, my subjective or unconscious emotional contents could be met, explored, felt, witnessed, metabolized, and integrated. Over time he began to encourage me to embrace my activist, to be more proactive as a way to engage with my environmental anxiety and despair. The work was life-changing, and I eventually (many years later) became certified as a Jungian analyst, greatly influenced by this early experience of an interpersonal, two-person analysis.

For me, working on what felt like opposites was an inner drive to find a relationship between the field of science with the field of analysis. While difficult, there have been many benefits to walking two paths. By giving voice to what Jung (1985, CW-16, ¶180) described as a man's philosophy of life, his psychic dominant, or what I have imagined as remembering the Nature archetype, my inner activist could emerge as an analytic third thing, as also a symbolic image for that which both holds and expresses both poles. To avoid becoming one-sided and engaging in unconscious splitting, both the scientist and the relational therapist (left and right brain) required "more integrative, mature and authentic modes of engagement with environmental issues that may involve, but are not predicated on, 'splitting' in the sense of cutting up the world into discrete and concrete objects (Lertzman, 2015, p. 132)." Lertzman emphasizes that through exploring our ambivalence and complicated emotions, we eventually discover a maturity that I believe can foster the energy of the activist that is both internally and externally directed.

What I experience in my consulting room is that by deliberately working with the Nature archetype and the associated shadow content that is often wordless or disavowed, Jung's concept of a unifying symbol offers a pathway towards a moment of change and fertilizes a growing consciousness. For instance, a male analysand had the following dream:

He was with two others camping in a forest and became frightened by a bear that walked into their campsite while they were cooking burgers on a campfire. He climbed a tree to escape (in reality—an awfully bad survival strategy) and watched as the bear took a burger from the heavy grill over the hot fire. The bear burned its hand and kicked at the fire, which set the brush alight.

Associations to the dream were his own environmental and climate anxiety. "I was up a tree, with a bear waiting for me and the world catching fire around me." He noted it described how he felt in his life. "No one will save us from this climate problem." He expressed his anxiety, grief, and despair yet understood that nature is enraged. It is noteworthy that he did not immediately associate the bear to his personal mother, or to the conflict he was having with his family at the time, although we later discussed this as one possibility.

I thought of my own working through process, the internal work of unpacking the feeling of futility, grief, and depression, which led to a 'vaccination' or sense of psychic immunity from working 'in the field' with personal and collective climate anxiety that arises from environmental contamination traumas. My 'inoculations' include high-conflict and emotional situations like managing public meetings or talking with and visiting residents whose homes have been contaminated and are now perhaps unlivable. This process helps with my analysand's working-through process.

Through my own shadow work, I discovered how the activist allows for the emotional experience to be present while encouraging the airing of conflicts and supportive dialogue that led to collaborative planning sessions and problem-solving. Having become more comfortable with expressing my own vulnerabilities, I was better able to tolerate the affect of people most impacted by environmental damage. I have found that my patience and ability to listen has led to a certain amount of repair following the intense ruptures with expressions of grief and discord (Tronick and Gold, 2020). After all, psychoanalysis, Jungian analysis, and eco-psychology are all forms of subversive activism simply because they support an individual to find and hold their own mind, to listen to the layers of emotions, to their unconscious, to their own inner nature, and to, at some point, find a way to express their views in a world that may reject them. They encourage individuation over conformity. "Where the Nature archetype is concerned, our experiences are so deeply embedded, or so deeply rooted in the human psyche, and our internal conflict is often so strong that it is debilitating for us to speak out" but it is often the power of the group that can "provide an effective counterweight" to the archetypal defenses (Foster, 2011, pp. 94–95). Although we recognize and understand personal trauma, we rarely specifically acknowledge how our personal trauma intersects with environmental and climate collapse. The intersection includes exploring feelings of love and guilt, where the

> struggle with nature is . . . partly felt to be a struggle to *preserve nature*, because it also expresses the wish to make reparation to her (mother).

People who strive with the severity of nature thus not only take care of themselves, but also serve nature herself.

(Klein, 1946/1975, pp. 337–338)

In the earlier dream, the bear's expression of rage forced the client to also consider his own guilt and how he might access the activist that could initiate some repair.

Another theory that supports denial and a lack of action is the persecutor/protector self-care system (Kalsched, 1996), which protects against the feelings associated with traumatic events and denies the possibility of resolving reenactments triggered by traumatic environmental events. These unseen traumas stir powerful emotions in the unconscious because they activate the unacknowledged aspect of a split described in Jung's 1961 essay. In *Healing the Split*, Jung (1977, CW-18, ¶578–607) made the statement that humanity's "immediate communication with nature is gone forever, and the emotional energy it generated has sunk into the unconscious" (Jung, 1977, CW-18, ¶585). Jung described symptoms related to the loss of connection with nature, such as a loss of numinosity, the collapse of moral and spiritual tradition, a sense of isolation and feeling alone. These symptoms are not unlike those discussed by Edinger (1972, pp. 56–57), when referring to a rupture in the ego-Self axis: psychosomatic symptoms, attacks of primitive affect, depression, suicidal impulses, existential anxiety, and an unconscious sense worthlessness. Likewise, rupture or split in the ego-Nature axis would accompany the rupture in the individual's ego-Self axis. In other words, psychologically, when looking at the ego-Nature axis, with nature as an aspect of the archaic Self, we maintain, restore, or repair our psychological health and become more resilient through cultivating a conscious relationship with the ego-Nature axis. More recently, the use of psilocybin mushrooms has been shown to increase nature relatedness and decrease depression as well as authoritarian political views (Lyons and Carhart-Harris, 2018; Foster, 2019). In effect, this use of nature to heal our own nature is gaining respect in contemporary medical and psychological settings.

Fear of Nature

Based on humanity's origins in nature, which millennia ago was both a nurturing and hostile environment, it is not surprising that our unconscious may view nature as dangerous. As Klein (1946/1975) points out, we have both loving and destructive impulses that require recognition if we are ever able to shift our attitudes. The origins of such feelings are the likely source of our fear of nature (von Franz, 1972), which indeed has archaic roots associated with survival. Consequently, our desire to control nature may stem from this fear and is evidenced in some reactions to the recent pandemic. Within the context of this paper, attitudes towards the COVID-19 pandemic, vaccinations, mask wearing (or not), and human-environment interactions reflect the presence of the Nature archetype in its most destructive form, forcing humanity to become conscious of its vulnerability to nature's unpredictability and uncertainty.

Specifically, the recent coronavirus (CoV) is reported to be the result of a zoonotic spillover, the name given when a disease found in non-human species, such as bats, pigs, or chickens, crosses into humans, causing disease, or even a pandemic (Quammen, 2013). In the past 20 years, there have been three new sudden acute respiratory syndrome (SARS) virus-strain outbreaks: the SARS CoV outbreak in 2004 (Vijayanand and Woodhead, 2004); the Middle East respiratory syndrome (MERS) outbreak in 2014 (van den Bland *et al.*, 2015); and the SARS-CoV-2 outbreak (Bael et al., 2020). All deadly, and all the result of "spillover" from the dark recesses of nature. These diseases reinforce an archaic fear of nature, and within the broader concept of nature, these diseases stimulate a certain type of nature trauma reflected by unconscious collective depression and dissociation.

Environmental Trauma

The climate crisis and its related trauma has intersecting issues that include, but are not limited to, environmental injustice and toxic trauma from hazardous waste, and when viewed through a neurobiology lens, climate and environmental challenges activate six of the nervous system's seven core emotions identified by Panskepp (2012a, 2012b): fear, rage, care, grief, play, seeking, and lust.

The *logos*, or logic, that defends against important complexes derived from archetypal structures related to nature, such as home and food security, and fear of harm from the unseen and unknown (Foster, 2011), are finally being taken seriously, as shown by the APA's admissions. The residual trauma caused by years of anxiety over environmental problems are only just beginning to surface. Even more poignant is the fact that environmental anxiety has been running in the background or our postmodern lives like a 'resident virus' on the hard drive of our brains, using up computing power and tying up our primary software. It is no wonder that when COVID-19 added additional anxiety and pressure to the system, it caused glitches, hang-ups, and crashes of our emotional operating systems. Our subjective experiences became overwhelming. Our psychological knowledge became useful in working with our environmental problems, even though it meant balancing the complexity with the continued diligence on a local level (Winter and Koger, 2004, p. 232).

Psychological Multiplicity

Jung's notion that multiplicity within the psyche is a natural, non-pathological phenomenon is becoming more recognized and accepted as providing flexibility in the mind, and a way to engage with our vulnerabilities while in relationship with one another. Within the relational framework of a Jungian analysis, when confronting environmental trauma and its companion complexes, such as those activated by the climate emergency and waste dumping, analysts need to be not just trauma-informed therapists but also climate-informed, which includes an awareness of emotions that arise from environmental destruction or ecological contamination and extinction fears that may remain invisible yet ubiquitously present.

Analysts recognize that some complexes, such as early childhood trauma or addiction, stretch deep into the layers of the psyche because they are rooted in relational or archetypal energies connected with the instinctual seeking system associated with life and death, safety, security, food, reproduction, etc. (Panksepp, 2012b). Similarly, the analyst is called to understand the issues that activate their inner activist and what leads to an avoidance of this energy. When the spirit is aroused, the activist shows itself through strong opinions and recommendations. However, analysis requires empathically and collaboratively exploring emotions, associations, images, and experience with analysands rather than rigidly adhering to an opinion. As with early trauma, these complexes can be found in and released from the body using techniques such as EMDR, Brainspotting®, and other body-centered modalities. By working with the somatic unconscious, connecting, or probing mind-body connections, the body becomes a vessel that expresses nature itself, and the ego-Nature axis is further deepened by the fact that we breathe and have emotions. So where do these modalities, Jungian analysis, and activism fit together?

At the beginning of Jung's CW-17, McGuire (1954) states that the "conscious realization . . . [of] . . . individuation is the aim of human development in the second half of life." And that "no account of individuation, therefore, would be complete without a psychological outline of the early formative period of development." This suggests that individuation is better realized by the person if they have worked on [analyzed] their early-life complexes. In our rapidly changing environmental world, an individual who comes to analysis because of an environmental complex or trauma would be in a situation where current and early childhood environmental issues are likely comorbid. Working with environmental trauma or environmental complexes retrieves memories of early play in nature; connections with fish, frogs, animals, and ecological environments of the past loaded with powerful emotions and images that perhaps only had surfaced in dreams. Through this vulnerable and tender work, the I-Nature relationship is uncovered during the analysis, and it contains the somatic memories and tactile sensations of nature of *then and now* images (water, mud, wind, and sun, etc.).

As described by Mitchell (2020), Jacobi (1965) and Edinger (1972) observed that a lifelong interactive ego-Self relationship is required for individuation and adaptation (CW-9ii, ¶45–47). These analysts proposed a solution to the analyst's dilemma in the form of Developmental Individuation, which pays attention to preserving the ego-Self axis while helping the ego's adaptation to outer reality, leading to the stabilization of the ego without breaking the ego-Self axis. The ego is differentiated from the Self, though the connection is maintained through the process of sublimating the archaic, magical, and mythical structures of consciousness.

Analysands who suffer the angst of separation from the nature aspect of the Self may be more highly activated when confronted by disruptions that relate to nature and the outer world. From an eco-psychology perspective, we may notice more analysands with a ruptured ego-Nature axis that leads to symptoms related to the split that Jung referred to when writing about our separation from nature "depression, suicidal impulses, existential anxiety, and an unconscious sense worthlessness."

While working to restore and strengthen early damage to the ego-Self axis, we have choices about how we work within the analysis, hence the Jungian dilemma. Do we actively work with the symbolic material opening to the broader world of nature and the Self, or do we work with the emotions related to nature that are being processed by the ego, or do we do both? Where the activist is concerned, we may work with early memories that relate to the Nature archetype such as safety in the home or immediate environment, and security related to health, food, and survival. Difficult feelings are exacerbated by a lack of control of one's own environment and issues of fairness and justice related to the politics of hazardous waste, chemical facility siting, and environmental regulation and policing, which reflect ruptures in trust, power differentials, and evoke feelings of abandonment.

Both Jung and Edinger played an active role in the analysis of their analysands, and both brought their conscious and unconscious selves into the analysis. Edinger notes:

> The more deeply one considers the matter, the more it seems that in effective psychotherapy, patient and therapist are participating in a dynamic field of the objective psyche, which they share jointly. This way of viewing the psychotherapeutic process seems more conducive to successful therapy than the notion of projection, which tends to throw the patient back on himself and neglects the reality of the participating analyst.
>
> (p. 78)

It is no surprise that today's neuropsychology and attachment research reaffirm this point of view with the imaginative right-brain-to-right-brain model (McGilchrist, 2009; Schore, 2019). The work with ego-Nature axis ruptures is supported by Edinger's (2002) analytic process that strengthens the ego-Self axis, serving the individuation process, which is needed more than ever to bring consciousness to current earth crisis.

The Self as Activist

Jung's concept of the Self is complex (Jung, 1979, CW-9ii, ¶43–68), but the ego's relationship to the Self was developed by Jung because of his appreciation for the deeper transpersonal aspects of the psyche as a guiding and expansive principle. In most simple terms, the Self allows for the presence of something larger in our lives than personal ego consciousness and recognizes the teleological unfolding of our life's journey. It is a search for depth and wholeness (Jung, 1979, CW-9ii, ¶490) and perhaps, as Fellows (2019, 2020) emphasizes, working towards a *metanoia* regarding our relationship with nature. From a Freudian perspective, the super ego cannot save us from our climate crisis that is becoming more forceful with damages that affect our survival. Moreover, perhaps the Christian myth no longer works because we (humans) neither take responsibility for our impact on the earth nor embrace the power of our own progressive energy for innovation and renewal. That is, we no longer feel the need to take responsibility for our sins against the earth but wait to be absolved of these sins in the afterlife, and defer to others to take responsibility.

When one looks at the development of Jung's work and realizes that it spans the discovery of the unconscious, his personal journeying that resulted in *The Red Book* (Jung, 2009), the whirlwinds of the first World War, the rise of Nazism (1933 through 1945), and the initiation of the atomic era, one can see that Jung was himself not just individuating but was *adapting* to vast changes within the collective. While he made blunders and was imperfect in some of his choices, he was an activist in support of the unconscious, navigating difficult historic moments through the promotion of his new psychology. His various thoughts on the role of the Self in guiding individual lives reflected his own psychic development but most certainly served as an inspiration for how we might continue the myth forward (Jung, 1979, CW-9ii, ¶ 43–67). Jung's interrelated active analysis, that we refer to as a two-person model, sitting face-to-face, and the work of Edinger and Jacobi all suggest that the activist and its subsequent progressive energy of activism is necessary to some degree in analysis and, as a result, must be made conscious in relationship to Jung's notion of the prospective psyche. And, given our planet's current plight, which no doubt is due in part to the level of personal and collective destructive energies, discord, and rupture we see in our analysand's ego-Nature axis, we are left with limited time to confront the challenges expressed by the climate emergency and the environmental crisis that mirrors our own dissociative internal splits away from our own true nature and nature itself. It is time to ask where does our activist show itself, and how may it honorably be revived to serve and to heal the human-Nature rupture?

References

APA. (2009a). *Psychology and Global Climate Change: Addressing a Multi-faceted Phenomenon and Set of Challenges, a Report by the American Psychological Association's Task Force on the Interface Between Psychology and Global Climate Change*, American Psychological Association, www.apa.org/science/about/publications/climate-change.aspx

APA. (2009b). *Policy Recommendations of the APA Task Force on the Interface Between Psychology and Global Climate Change*, American Psychological Association, www.apa.org/science/about/publications/climate-change.aspx

APA. (2011). *Resolution on Affirming Psychologists' Role in Addressing Global Climate Change*, www.apa.org/science/about/publications/climate-change

APA. (2017). *Resource Document on Mental Health and Climate Change*, Edited by Robert J. Ursano, Joshua C. Morganstein, and Robin Cooper, www.apa.org/about/governance/climate-change-task-force

APA. (2019). *Confronting the Climate Crisis*, Edited by Kirsten Weir, 1 November, www.apa.org/monitor/2019/11/climate-crisis

Bael, Kee Baek, Woong, Sohn, Soo-Yeon, Mahgoub, Ahmed, and Hage, Robert. (2020). A comprehensive review of severe acute respiratory syndrome coronavirus 2. *Cureus*, 12(5): e7943, doi:10.7759/cureus.7943

Barsness, Roy. (2018). *Core Competencies of Relational Analysis: A Guide to Practice, Study and Research*, Routledge, New York, NY.

Buber, Martin. (1970). *I and Thou*, Charles Scribner's Sons, New York, NY.

Carson, Rachel. (1962). *Silent Spring*, Houghton Mifflin Company, New York, NY.

Carson, Rachel. (2021). *The Life and Legacy*, Crown, New York.

Cwik, August. (2011). Associative dreaming: Reverie and active imagination. *Journal of Analytical Psychology*, 56(1): 14–36.

Edinger, Edward. (1972). *Ego and Archetype*, Shambhala Press, Boston.

Edinger, Edward. (2002). *Science of the Soul: A Jungian Perspective*, Inner City Press, Toronto, ON.

Fellows, Andrew. (2019). *Gaia, Psyche and Deep Ecology: Navigating Climate Change in the Anthropocene*, Routledge, New York, NY.

Fellows, Andrew. (2020). Irreducible responsibility to navigate the Anthropocene. In *Holism: Possibilities and Problem*, Edited by Christian McMillian, Rodrick Main, and David Henderson, Routledge, New York, NY.

Foster, Stephen. (2011). *Risky Business; A Jungian View of Environmental Disasters and the Nature Archetype*, Inner City Press, Toronto, ON.

Foster, Stephen. (2012). In my back yard; legacies of the American West. *Environmental Disasters and Collective Trauma, Spring Books and Journals*, 88.

Foster, Stephen. (2019). Nature as other: Separation and reconnection in an ever-changing world. In *Proceedings of the International Association of Analytical Psychology*, pp. 216–220, Vienna.

Foster, Stephen. (2022). Eco-anxiety in everyday life: facing the anxiety and fear of a degraded Earth in analytic work. *Journal of Analytical Psychology*, 67(5): 1363–1385.

Hill, Julia Butterfly. (1999). *The Legacy of Luna: The Story of a Tree, a Woman, and the Struggle to Save the Redwoods*, https://juliabutterflyhill.com/shop/

Jacobi, Jolanda. (1965). *The Way of Individuation*, Harcourt Brace Jovanovich, New York, NY.

Jung, Carl G. (1961). *Memories, Dreams, Reflections*, Random House, New York, NY.

Jung, Carl G. (1977). Healing the split. In *The Symbolic Life*, Collected Works Volume 18, Princeton University Press, Princeton, NJ.

Jung, Carl G. (1979). Christ as a symbol of the self. In *Aion: Researches into the Phenomenology of the Self Psychotherapy*, Collected Works Volume 9ii, Princeton University Press, Princeton, NJ.

Jung, Carl G. (1985). Psychology and a philosophy of life. In *The Practice of Psychotherapy*, Collected Works Volume 16, Princeton University Press, Princeton, NJ.

Jung, Carl G. (2009). *Liber Novus*, Philemon Foundation and W. W. Norton & Co., New York, NY.

Kalsched, Donald. (1996). *The Inner World of Trauma: Archetypal Defenses of the Personal Spirit*, Routledge, New York, NY.

Keating, Thomas. (1999). *The Human Condition: Contemplation and Transformation*, Paulist Press, New York, NY.

Kimbles, Samuel. (2016). Phantom narratives, a framework for cultural activism in the consulting room. In *Analysis and Activism; Social and Political Contributions of Jungian Psychology*, Edited by Emilija Kiehl, Mark Saban, and Andrew Samuels, Routledge, London and New York, NY.

Klein, Melanie. (1946/1975). Love, guilt and reparation (1937). In *Love, Guilt and Reparation and Other Works 1921–1945*, Vol. I. pp. 306–343, The Free Press, MacMillan, Inc., New York, NY.

Kolbert, Elizabeth. (2014). *The Sixth Extinction: An Unnatural History*, Henry Holt and Company, New York, NY.

Lertzman, Renee. (2015). *Environmental Melancholia, Psychoanalytic Dimensions of Engagement*, Routledge, New York, NY.

Lovelock, James E., and Margulis, Lynn. (1974). Atmospheric homeostasis by and for the biosphere-The Gaia hypothesis. *Tellus* 26(1): 2–10. Bibcode 1974Tell . . . 26 . . . . 2L, doi:10.1111/j.2153-3490.1974.tb01946.x

Lyons, Taylor, and Carhart-Harris, Robin. (2018). Increased nature relatedness and decreased authoritarian political views after psilocybin for treatment-resistant depression. *Journal of Psychopharmacology*, 32(7): 811–819.

Mann, Michael E. (2021). *The New Climate War: The Fight to Take Back Our Planet*, Hachette Book Group, New York, NY.

Maroda, Karen. (1991). *The Power of Countertransference: Innovations in Analytic Techniques*, The Analytic Press, New York, NY.

McGilchrist, Iain. (2009). *The Master and His Emissary: The Divided Brain and the Making of the Western World*, Yale University Press, New Haven, CT.

McGuire, William. (1954). *Development of Personality*, Editor's note on C.G. Jung, Collected Works, Volume 17, Princeton University Press, Princeton, NJ.

McKibben, Bill. (2021). *Official Site for Bill McKibben: Author-Educator-Environmentalist*, https://billmckibben.com/

Meares, Russell, Butt, David, Henderson-Brooks, Caroline, and Samir, Hany. (2005). A poetics of change. *Psychoanalytic Dialogs*, 676.

Mitchell, Robert. (2020). Holistic education: The Jungian dilemma. In *Holism: Possibilities and Problems*, Edited by Christian McMillan, Roderick Main, and David Henderson, Routledge, London and New York, NY.

Næss, Arne. (1989). *Ecology, Community and Lifestyle*, Cambridge University Press, Cambridge.

Orange, Donna. (2017). *Climate CRISIS, Psychoanalysis, and Radical Ethics*, Routledge, New York, NY.

Panksepp, Jaak. (2012a). *The Archaeology of Mind: Neuroevolutionary Origins of Human Emotions*, WW Norton and Company, New York, NY.

Panksepp, Jaak. (2012b). Affective neuroscience of the emotional BrainMind: Evolutionary perspectives and implications for understanding depression. *Dialogues in Clinical Neuroscience* (2010 December), 12(4): 533–545, doi:10.31887/DCNS.2010.12.4/jpanksepp

Quammen, David. (2013). *Spillover: Animal Infections and the Next Human Pandemic*, Norton & Company, London.

Samuels, Andrew. (2014). Political and clinical developments in analytical psychology, 1972–2014: Subjectivity, equality and diversity—inside and outside the consulting room. *Journal of Analytical Psychology*, 59(5): 641–660.

Samuels, Andrew. (2017). The "activist client": Social responsibility, the political self, and clinical practice in psychotherapy and psychoanalysis. *Psychoanalytic Dialogues*, 27(6): 678–693.

Schore, Allan. (2019). *Right Brain Psychotherapy*, W.W. Norton and Company, New York, NY.

Searles, Harold. (1972). Unconscious processes in relation to the environmental crisis. *Psychoanalytic Review*, 59: 361–374.

Thunberg, Greta. (2021). *Greta Thunberg—Wikipedia*, https://en.wikipedia.org/wiki/Greta_Thunberg

Tronick, Ed, and Gold, Claudia. (2020). *The Power of Discord: Why the Ups and Downs of Relationship Are the Secret to Building Intimacy, Resilience, and Trust*, Little Brown Spark, New York, NY, Boston, MA and London.

van den Bland, Judith M. A., Smits, Saskia L., and Haagmans, Bart L. (2015). Pathogenesis of Middle East respiratory syndrome coronavirus. *Pathology*, 235(2): 175–184.

Vijayanand, Pandurangan, and Woodhead, Mark. (2004). Severe acute respiratory syndrome (SARS): A review of Pandurangan Vijayanand, Ed Wilkins, and Mark Woodhead. *Clinical Medicine*, 4(2): 152–160.

Von Franz, Marie-Louise. (1972). *Creation Myth*, Spring Publications, Zurich, Switzerland.

Weintrobe, Sally. (2021). *Psychological Roots of the Climate Crisis*, Bloomsbury Academic Publishing, London.

Wilkerson, Isabel. (2020). *Caste: The Origins of Our Discontents*, Random House, New Nork, NY.

Winter, D. N. D., and Koger, S. M. (2004). *The Psychology of Environmental Problems*, 2nd ed., Lawrence Erlbaum Associates Publishers, Mahwah, NJ.

Wohl, Ellen. (2016). *Key Figures: North American Environmental Scientist Activists*, doi:10.1093/OBO/9780199363445-0062; www.oxfordbibliographies.com/view/document/obo-9780199363445/obo-9780199363445-0062.xml

Chapter 2

Archetypal Nonviolence in Analysis

Renée M. Cunningham

This analytic exploration will circumambulate archetypal nonviolence and its role in developing consciousness within the individual and culture. Utilizing Jungian analytical psychology, archetypal nonviolence will be defined and amplified by examining the racial complex and the emergent phenomenon of nonviolence in response to violence and oppression inherent in the complex. Nonviolent activism plays an integral role in the process of shadow integration as the personality unfolds individually and within the conceptual framework of community. Therefore, it is vital to explore how the philosophical ethos of nonviolence may serve as a collective unifier and cultivator of peace. This can be understood by examining how archetypal nonviolence unfolds within the individual in the consulting room as an integral aspect of the individuation process and subsequently affects the outer world.

Civil nonviolent activism has been a pivotal force in the archetypal experience of democracy in America, one that continuously informs the shaping of the nation. Utilizing the George Floyd murder as the flashpoint for the current uprising in America, I will discuss and amplify how violent upheavals within the collective are being mediated through the compensatory phenomenon of archetypal nonviolence. Emergent collective phenomena representing the *coniunctio* between violence and nonviolence in the summer of 2020 resulted in the Capitol Hill Autonomous Zone (CHAZ) and Athena of Portland, to name a few. Similarly, within the context of analysis, symbols emerge within the archetypal field as the analyst holds the tension between nonviolent (conscious) and violent (unconscious) psychic forces.

Archetypal nonviolence enters the consulting room of every analyst. The constellation of complexes reveals the source of the patient's suffering. Suffering, the tincture to the transmutation of psychic energy, must be tolerated

DOI: 10.4324/9781003252993-3

and integrated by both parties if the patient is to feel better. But this entails the analyst experiencing the patient's psyche while also being mindful of their own landmines. The opportunity for consciousness and subsequent change in behavior occurs when the analyst refuses to collude with the complex through an emergent, organic, nonviolent intervention.

In considering any analysis, the analyst must also understand the role culture plays in the patient's life. Like religious influences, cultural complexes contain the striations of culturally defined unconscious materials which influence a patient's beliefs and constructed defenses around said beliefs. Indeed, it is difficult to separate the individual from the cultural context within which they live. When treating the patient, the analyst is effectively, unconsciously, treating the problems in culture as well.

Psychoanalyst and object relations theorist Ronald Fairbairn (1935) contends that "all sociological problems are ultimately reducible to problems of individual psychology" (p. 241). Jungian scholar Andrew Samuels (1993), who writes extensively on the political psyche, states,

> The political tasks of modern democracy are similar to the psychological tasks of modern therapy and analysis. In both areas, there is a fight between consciousness, liberation and alterity on the one hand and suppression, repression and omnipotent beliefs in final truths on the other. Psychological and political processes share an uncertain outcome. Hence, the demarcation between the inner world of psychology and the outer world of politics has no permanent existence. The *unwelt* is both inside and outside.
>
> (p. 4)

Transformation, then, relies on the individual's capacity to develop a life of consciousness which can then effectively change the outer world as well. Analysis offers the patient the opportunity to change the outer world through the transmuting of their inner world. This process begins with the analyst guiding the way through the weekly metaphorical marches of activism, with the patient desiring relief from the oppressive forces which they are convinced lives outside of themselves. The analyst holds the potential to introduce the patient to their inner other, whom they do not know but who blocks their way to freedom. This inner world of oppression can then be addressed, a light shining on the interiority of the patient's shadow through the analyst's nonviolent ethos. When the patient can surrender to the inner violence through nonviolent shadow integration, their world may begin to change.

Archetypal Nonviolence

One of the earliest literary exposés on nonviolence comes from Percy Shelley, an early nineteenth-century writer who penned *The Mask of Anarchy*. Published in 1932, the poem was composed as a response to the Peterloo Massacre of 1819 in England. Shelley understands that the power of nonviolence can shift the forces of violence for the good of the collective. He interprets slavery as an inner and outer condition, defined by oppression, inflicted upon a segment of society that is marginalized by the powerful. The victims of violence who have become shells of themselves are encouraged to wake up to the abuse and unite in number against the oppressor:

> Rise like Lions after slumber
> In unvanquishable number,
> Shake your chains to earth like dew
> Which in sleep had fallen on you -
> Ye are many—they are few.
>
> What is Freedom?—ye can tell
> That which slavery is, too well -
> For its very name has grown
> To an echo of your own.
>
> 'Tis to work and have such pay
> As just keeps life from day to day
> In your limbs, as in a cell
> For the tyrants' use to dwell,
>
> So that ye for them are made
> Loom, and plough, and sword, and spade,
> With or without your own will bent
> To their defense and nourishment.
>
> (Shelley, P.B. *The Mask of Anarchy*,
> p. 38, Kindle edition)

Shelley's moving verses arose from a life defined by oppression and abuse. Through his suffering, Shelly learned to catalyze his aggression into change for the better, ultimately leaving his immortal mark on the generations that followed through his writing, his agony shaping his becoming through the wisdom of his suffering. Shelley's suffering inspired his activism, his writings movingly depicting the nonviolent uprising which tipped the scales of justice in nineteenth-century England. His life of activism demonstrates the nature of Jung's idea of the archetype of individuation: individuation unfolds as an individual grapples with the demands between the inner and outer worlds in the drive to become *uniquely* fully human. Shelley's life and work reflect this process.

Author Mark Kurlansky, in his book *Nonviolence: The History of a Dangerous Idea* (2006), states that "while every major language has a word for violence, there is no word to express the idea of nonviolence" (p. 5). "It is a state of mind and heart that directly addresses violence by using thought, word, and deed in such a way as to dissolve, break apart, and transmute violence from chaos to ordered energy" (Cunningham, 2020, p. 35).

Gandhi (1962) observes/notes that the closest terminology to nonviolence comes from the Sanskrit word *Ahimsa*. "*Ahimsa* is a derivative of the word himsa, which means to harm. . . . Important to Hinduism and Buddhism, *Ahimsa* is the complete absence of violence in word and even though as well as action" (p. xxv). *Ahimsa* is a philosophical, spiritual stance that is evolutionary in nature and can never truly be achieved (Kurlansky, 2006; Gandhi, 1962). "Nonviolence is a perfect stage. It is a goal towards which all humanity moves naturally, though unconsciously" (Gandhi, 1962, p. xxv).

Gandhi referred to consciousness as *Satyagraha*. "*Satyagraha*—literally 'holding on to Truth'—is the name he coined for his method of fighting without violence or retaliation" (Gandhi, 1962, p. xxiv). The application of *Satyagraha* supports consciousness and counteracts the influence(s) of evil.

> It means that evil is real only insofar as we support it. The essence of holding on to truth is to withdraw support of what is wrong. If enough people do this from a great enough depth—evil has to collapse from lack of support.
>
> (p. xxiv)

Satyagraha provides the *active* (process of consciousness) activism in nonviolent philosophy, whereas *Ahimsa* supports the study and practice of nonviolence to self and other. "*Ahimsa* is unconditional love"; *Satyagraha* is love in action.

While Gandhi did not support violence, he detested pacifism even more, for he viewed it as a potential impetus to violence. "There is hope for a violent man to become nonviolent. There is no such hope for the impotent" (Kurlansky, p. 149). *Satyagraha*, or truth force, can meet violence through the assertion of will. As a spiritual practice, nonviolence can be as forceful as violence and contains the potential to shift the spiritual landscape within an individual or culture.

In the Chinese language, the word closest to nonviolence is *teh*. "In Taoism, there is a concept embodied in the *teh*. Not exactly nonviolence, which is an active force, *teh* is the virtue of not fighting—nonviolence is the path to *teh*" (Kurlansky, 2006, p. 11). Ultimately, *teh*, like *Ahimsa*, is a state that cannot be perfected but can be pursued through a path of nonviolence. Nonviolence, and its activism, may come with harsh psychic blows or be subtly implemented through the Taoist concept of *Wu Wei*. Jungian analyst Ursula Wirtz, in her book *Trauma and Beyond* (2021), describes nonviolent psychic tension as a hovering of attention:

> In Jungian therapy, Freud's 'evenly hovering attention' is blended with the paradoxical Taoist "wu wei" principle. Wu Wei, the action of nonaction, is a feminine principle that refers to *spontaneous action* that arises from the center of being not from the ego but from the creative powers of instinct. Wu Wei is described as a soft yielding, not resisting the flow, a kind of vigilant passivity. The attitude of letting things be, in which in the being is the doing, engenders diverse modes of awareness, including imagination, intuition, and sensory perception, modes that are extremely important for an analyst working with trauma.
>
> (p. 155)

According to Kurlansky (2006), the one word that comes closest to nonviolence is the Islamic term *jihad*, which means "nonviolent activism." In the Quran, the term *jihad* "originally meant to strive with great intensity for a relationship with Allah. However, this striving was supposed to be an internal struggle to become the perfect Muslim that God-Allah wanted each Muslim to be" (p. 36). Unfortunately, in the term *jihad*, the paradigm of the internal struggle is misunderstood as an outer goal of converting the other to Islam in the name of Allah/God. In its essence, however, the word *jihad* supports the journey of nonviolent activism and inner ethic, which mirrors the process of psychological individuation (p. 36). According to Mairead Corrigan Maguire, in *Peace is the Way*,

> Gandhi realized that the spirit of nonviolence begins within us and moves out from there. The life of nonviolence is the fruit of an inner peace and spiritual unity already realized in us and not the other way around. . . . Herein lies the power of nonviolence. As our hearts are disarmed by God of our inner violence, they become God's instruments for the disarmament of the world.
>
> (p. 159)

According to Fabrizio Petri, in his article "Gandhi, Jung and Nonviolence Today" (2014), *Ahimsa*, the practice of nonviolent love, is an interpersonal commitment to transform the inner and outer worlds, "to innovate entirely without revolution, and to deeply transform the present without disregarding the past" (p. 8). Nonviolence submits a new ethic that offers all participants of the violent paradigm something other than oppression, dominance, and humiliation, for nonviolence deeply affects all parties involved. It addresses the fundamental rupture in the paradigm of relationship, either intrapsychically, between the ego and the Self, or, in the outer world, with another. Nonviolence returns the marginalized back into the folds of community.

Nonviolence in Analysis

At the core of any analysis is relationship building, brought to bear on both parties through discovering one's Self emerging through moment-to-moment encounters with the other in the analytic hour. The inner other consists of the unconscious, subjective psychological and emotional experiences shaped by object relations affected by culture, class, race, religion, and sexual or gender identity. Psychoanalyst Julie Davies, in her article "Cultural Dimensions of Intersubjectivity" (2011), explains: "The challenge of authentically knowing our patients, or ourselves, is immense. Whether culturally or racially similar or different, we are each subjectively unique, and encountering 'otherness' is therefore central to the analytic endeavor" (p. 550). Holding these differences invariably brings conflict and is an essential element of understanding one another and the process of inner knowing. Davies further observed,

> In psychoanalysis, it appears that the effort to connect with the 'other' is as psychologically transforming to both participants as the achievement of understanding. The process of trying to apprehend the subjectivity of another is complex, unpredictable, and when successful is inevitably altering to both patient and analyst.
>
> (p. 550)

Both the effort and process comprise a form of nonviolent activism, a dynamic of coming into being with one's Self through the process of individuation as it occurs in the analytic experience. This inevitably means that we must face the darker aspects of the personality. According to Jungian analyst Pamela Power (2014), "whether one calls it shadow, trauma, resistance, destructiveness, envy, or narcissism, we [analysts] recognize that when we invite the forces for psychological growth, integration and individuation to manifest, we also invite the forces of anti-growth, anti-individuation and anti-life" (p. 33). Nonviolence is an active activism that insists upon a more conscious way, which inevitably means that aggression will be called up for transformation. Rosemary Montagnon, cited earlier, describes aggression as a life force energy closer to love than hate:

> I believe that aggression—a word that etymologically means 'to move forward', 'to step towards urgently'—is separate and distinct from destructiveness. Its roots are located in and nearer to Eros, the life force, than to Thanatos, the death force. For as Stevens remarked, 'without aggression survival would be impossible, but survival also demands that aggression be constrained' (ibid., p. 227). Aggression is thus compatible with the ethologist's view of it' but apart from its protection and defense of physical survival it is also needed to ensure self-cohesion and self-maintenance, now and in the future.
>
> (Montagnon, 2005, pp. 28–29)

Trauma impacts one's overall sense of well-being, often leaving one feeling bereft, alone, numb, angry, and communally separated from a deeper wellspring of existential meaning. In analysis, the patient finds in the analyst someone who can hold their suffering in such a way as to enable them to make sense of their lives. Traumas rule the psychic reality which grows up and around the patient's wound(s). Patients develop ingenious defenses against re-experiencing traumatic losses. They enter treatment in order to sort through the one-sided, ego-oriented life resulting from the trauma. Nonviolence enables a bridge to form between the conscious and unconscious realms, introducing the patient to the split-off shadow aspects of themselves to which they need access in order to feel free or experience an inner sense of wellness. But shadow is painful and remains unconsciously repressed, split off from the ego.

In analysis, the analyst's witnessing of the inner persecutor and victim dyad (archetypal master-slave) is mediated with compassion, advocacy, and a search for a truth defined by consciousness. Truth force and love force, or *Satyagraha* and *Ahimsa*, respectively, are Mahatma Gandhi's two tenets that can inform the analytic mantle and the activism of a conscious life. These two tenets shape the container within which the alchemical transformation of the personality takes place.

Within the process of individuation, the patient is prompted by the unconscious to explore the reasons for their egoic suffering. As confessions ensue, the patient begins the first stage of analysis, the anamnesis. Within the anamnesis, complexes are exposed as well as the psychic splits associated with the complexes. The divisions between the self and other begin violently responding to the self's call for psychic reconciliation. The analyst must bear this tension while watching for information from the patient's unconscious, shaping the nonviolent intervention to be implemented. The archetypal image of the nonviolent intervention will emerge in the subjective third. Such tactics include the analytic interpretation, a moment of silence, and the holding of hope, praise, praying, and singing (analytic reverie).

Analytic enactments of the master/slave archetypal relationship set in motion the personal complexes of the patient as well as the cultural and family complexes that have shaped the patient's ego strength and sense of self. A personal sense of injustice that develops from trauma can quickly transmute from the perpetrator/victim, master/slave paradigm between the analyst and analysand, to a racist enactment. A racist enactment does not always involve skin color but, without exception, involves oppression and domination. An ego that cannot recognize the projective roots of oppression or racism consequently falls victim to the influences of racism in their culture. Analysis unearths the wound, where the origins of the projective material reside.

A Case

She is difficult to like. She loathes vulnerability but craves love. She is ruled by envy. She humiliates me with her words. She punishes me with her actions and seems to enjoy it. She argues about everything, such that opposition defines her. Indeed, she is ruled by the envious inner other who enslaves her goodness in an underground locker.

She challenges my capacity to sit deeply within myself. I find that I am in a constant state of hypervigilance, preparing for the next personal onslaught of criticisms: "You seem removed today, am I not interesting enough? (laughing). . . . Just joking" Or, "If you would listen, you would remember." She is consistently late for her appointments and has to be reminded to pay her invoice every month. These slights cloak the therapy in a mist of aggressive energy, hers and mine which obstruct my analytic vision. I know I am in trouble if I cannot drop deeper into the experience of myself.

I understand that with nonviolence I must separate my ego from her insults, but this is difficult to do without the capacity to put myself in her shoes. My ego wants to punish her with comments like: "Actually, *you* aren't any more interesting than you think I am." Or, the final insult, "At least I have an education!" With this thought I am shocked. I recognize the racist raise her ugly head. It has lethal potential. I think, feel myself pull back the reins and then a few more ideas pop in. I have thoughts of revenge like being late for her session or raising her fee. I catch this and soothe my bruised ego with the truth: "*Oooooh*, you are a really *mad* little snit!" I am in a power complex, and I need to check myself. I move into my body for a temperament check.

I am an exhausted analyst, filled with anxiety and frustration, anger at times seducing me into a hatred which I, with tremendous consciousness, must experience yet refuse refuge. All too often her inner persecutor finds my victim, and with her sadism she punishes me into withdrawal, all in a defense against trusting me. Even with my understanding and knowledge, my impatience can spill over into hatred, its ruthlessness strangling me, robbing me of my voice in the relationship. However, by holding my anger while reflecting on its inner source, I am at once informed of what she carries, what I carry, what we both carry. Through the door of the third I find a way in.

And I begin to remember the child who suffered and suffers.

She suffered whippings as a child, which wring her with acute physical anxiety and eating problems. She is humiliated daily by demons which define her introjects. She is fraught with the victimized vicissitudes of self-states created of past and present traumas, all ghostly hauntings, hauntings so palpable she is unable to hold partnership. This has impoverished her carnal and archetypal family life. Tragically, she is alone.

I know this is the time to move deeper into the images that reveal themselves to me in my anger. The images are courted by another side of pain that understands it must be held and not acted upon. Another layer of a desire for the way out via peace is also held. Ultimately, I know I can do nothing but work with my own suffering in order to come to an understanding. Nonviolent truth and suffering with and for the other is birthed through the shards of one's known shadow complex. It is only through the tincture of one's aggression that nonviolent consciousness can truly be achieved after a particularly difficult session. I hold my aggression throughout the day and into the night when I have the following dream. It takes place on a horizontal split screen:

> In the upper screen I see tanks and military armament being moved into position for war. I notice that the tanks are old, not as old as WWII and not modern, I assume they are Vietnam tanks, from the era in which my father served. In the lower screen, my sister appears (who died during Covid). I am so happy to see her. I ask her "is there a heaven where you are?" She smiles like the Mona Lisa. I chide her for her Cheshire grin. She states that indeed there is a heaven, and it is a lot like the carnal world, "but with no hassles of conflicts, or complexities like in real life. . . . It is very peaceful and serene." Another friend is there too, and she also states that there is a heaven. "It is hassle free; you know, like if you wanted to drive to Los Angeles, the traffic would be clear. No waiting, no jam ups. Really beautiful."

The dream conveys an archetypal level beneath the conscious, ego-driven realm. It is transcendent, the collective unconscious. In the Buddhist philosophy, this realm may be known as nirvana, "(in Buddhism) a transcendent state in which there is neither suffering, desire, where the subject is released from the effects of karma and the cycle of death and rebirth. It represents the final goal of Buddhism" (*Wikipedia*, 2023a). And while the dream is about heaven, it indicates that it is a realm accessible in carnal reality. While meditating on the dream, I begin imagining trading places with my patient and wonder what she might think about me, even within and under the envy. This informs me of my own undiscovered shadow. I begin asking myself questions: "Am I doing anything which may constellate her envy?" In my own frustrations, do I set up the hierarchical power structure of analyst and analysand in order to defend against my own anxieties or aggression? I imagine what her world might have been like in a childhood unprotected by her parents. Finally, I see myself in Selma with her in 1965, on that bridge on Bloody Sunday. The police are whipping her, and we are attempting to escape the violence. Surprisingly, I reach for her and guide her to shelter. I am moved by this imagery and find a new feeling of empathy and kinship leaking into my body. Mysteriously, I am released from my aggression, as a feeling of peace emerges. Suddenly, I am not so invested in my grudge, or hers. I understand how her inner world is being projected onto me as if I am a movie screen. But this is her inner reality, not mine. With this knowledge, my ego cuts the rope of an invested outcome.

She, however, has not moved off her dime. She strolls into the next session making a comment about my appearance: "Did you get your hair cut? I didn't think it could get any shorter." Riding in the slipstream of philosophical nonviolence is the analytic challenge, for it is within the present moment that its roots can be accessed and the subjective third can unfold. In a nonviolent stance, one holds affects of self and other in order to locate, if possible, an understanding, within disagreement and aggression. The analyst's devotion to Gandhi's concepts of *Ahimsa* and *Satyagraha* provides the context within this process, its consistent practice opening space for the elusive tao to emerge, or "the natural order of the universe" (*Wikipedia*, 2023b), within the analytic paradigm.

Taking in her comments, I sit quietly in my chair, leaning back, as if the comment has rocked me, which indeed it has. Suddenly the dream flashes through my mind. Minutes pass in silence. Finally, I find myself saying, "You know, I have been thinking about you over the past few days, and I've come to realize that for very good reasons, you don't seem to understand how your words affect people. . . . I am hurt by your words and I wonder if we can talk about it." Her eyes flash and then flicker with a sense of an awareness tinted with shame. Unable to tolerate such feeling, she throws her head back and sniffs the air. I feel as if she is re-loading her gun when suddenly her shoulders drop and she glances away. She sits in silence. I wait. Something feels like it might be clicking into order. "Well, you know I have a problem with my anger. You're supposed to be able to handle it." "I'd rather not," I say. "I'd rather *you* learn to handle it by telling me how you might be feeling, and then perhaps we could find the road map, together." After she hhrrumps at this, I ask, "I wonder if you are afraid of getting close to me, and so your comments, while they are hurtful, are meant to distance you from your true feelings." This lands too close. Her eyes turn into daggers from the interpretation; however, I sense an opening in between us, as the stillness expands the room, opening space for something new.

Spoon-feeding her bitterness back to her through nonviolent reflective listening lets her know that I understand her and can hold her aggressive feelings without it disintegrating both of us. I respond to her comments: "You feel as if I am not listening to you; however, I hear deeply that you need connection with me, and when you don't experience it then you feel rejected, and this stirs up feelings of alienation. I wonder if you have ever really felt heard." Her eyes widen at this truth. Her shoulders drop, and she sinks ever so slightly into the couch, this new relief giving way to an opening for the both of us. Consequently, I feel myself relax a bit too. This is a new breakthrough from months of volleys which have seemingly stalemated the relationship. Yet, even in the aggressiveness, I feel an opening within myself, signaling an opening in the humanity between the two of us. We have survived each other while subsequently making contact with our shared Self. This begins to chip away at some invisible barrier which has kept me living in the upper split screen of the dream, in the realm of artillery fire and tanks. Nonviolent interventions have surfaced from the transcendent realm, below the ego's defended position, as in the dream. Holding the tension with her enables me to access the lower realm or archetypal unconscious, where our shared humanity and the potential for dreaming and healing lives. Somewhere in the exchange and my reflective listening and mirroring, she learns that in her accusations of my not being present, she is not present because she is consumed by what she feels I have that she doesn't, and this keeps her locked in a place of anger and envy. These projections must be challenged throughout the treatment for they represent a fundamental deprivation in early childhood.

In her book *Projection and Re-collection in Jungian Psychology* (1995), Marie-Louise von Franz discusses the repeal of projective processes. Life organically offers one the opportunity for development. At the intersection of projection and re-collection, one is provided the opportunity to either reflect or turn away from consciousness. This intersection is where nonviolence emerges organically, offering the individual or culture the opportunity for moral or adaptive reconciliation between the inner and outer worlds:

> If one is caught in a projection that disturbs one's adaptation, whether it be an attraction full of fascination or hatred or obstinacy in clinging to a theory or an idea, at first one is carried along by a current of powerful affect as well as of desire or inner demand (to 'devour' the beloved object, to 'annhiliate' the enemy, to force the idea onto other people). This leads to behavior that is constantly at odds with the outer world, and conflicts and disappointments result. Pride and defiance then seduce one into a further struggle to push ahead in the same direction. . . . When the suffering has lasted long enough, so long that the ego and its strength are worn down and one begins to feel oneself to be 'small and ugly,' then at last comes that merciful moment when reflection is possible, when there is a reversal of the stream of energy, which now flows away from the object or the idea and toward oneself, or better still, toward the Self.
>
> (p. 162)

Repealing projections lies at the core of nonviolence and one's capacity for trust. Nonviolent listening reduces anxiety, holding open the door to inner reflection as trust builds. One builds upon the other, leading relationship building between self and other and, finally, community. Indeed, as nonviolence can transmute aggression within the individual, so it can within the culture as well.

Cultural Development Through Archetypal Nonviolence

Nonviolence serves the developmental process in social and political settings whereby systems have become morally corrupted by a one-sided attitude. Like the individual entering analysis to transform a life of suffering through a nonviolent pilgrimage, the marginalized or scapegoated, within the collective similarly march and protest the traumas borne from oppression in a supposedly free world. This communal reckoning is constructed organically through unification of the masses and a demand for justice, shining light on a moral adaptation crisis. Wars, protests, and violence often erupt moral discrepancies. Nonviolence enables a re-calibrating of the collective moral code.

In America, nonviolence as a sociopolitical ethos began as early as the 1940s. However, the Civil Rights Movement of the1950s and 1960s allowed for the archetypal experience of nonviolence to catch fire within the American psyche. Since the 2016 election, uprisings have flourished in such national campaigns as the #metoo movement, #timesup movement, and the #blacklivesmatter revolution of 2020–2021. However, these political, humanitarian efforts have been ushered in through the collective initiatory experience of the Women's March on Washington of 2017 and continued through the 2020 presidential election. With social media serving as an integral function of emerging collective consciousness, the nation's characterological problem of racism would once again surface with the murder of George Floyd, a black man from Minnesota.

On May 25, 2020, Eric Chauvin, a Minneapolis police officer, answered a radio call requesting backup for the arrest of George Floyd. The latter had attempted to pass a counterfeit twenty-dollar bill in a convenience store. A struggle to subdue Floyd ensued upon confronting him, but it was Officer Chauvin who had Floyd begging for his life, and in his last breaths, pleading for his mother. Floyd, handcuffed and pinned prone to the ground by three officers, could be seen struggling to breathe and break himself free of the police restraining him. In the last nine minutes and 26 seconds of Floyd's life, he announced he could not breathe 26 times. This seemed to matter little to Chauvin, who leaned on his neck and upper back, constricting his chest and oxygen flow, killing Floyd, his lungs and heart collapsing.

Primarily, people of color began gathering around the unfolding tragedy, many calling for the officers to let up, get off Floyd's neck, with panic-stricken pleas ending in anger and rage as the police officers did nothing to assist Floyd. As the scene escalated, Darnella Frazier, a 17-year-old black female, arriving on the scene, managed to pull out her phone camera, recording the entire event and subsequently posting it on Facebook. It is an interesting fact that while movements such as Gandhi's nonviolent revolution and Martin Luther King, Jr.'s civil rights campaigns were led by powerful men, it would be women like Maimie Till Bradley, Rosa Parks, and Darnella Frazier who would light the spark-to-bonfire change within their respective cultures.

The penetrating stare of Chauvin into the camera revealed the depravity buried deep within the personal complex of racism, his hatred resolute. Alone, this murder may have slipped between the headlines, yet another black man dead at the hands of police. However, this time the outcome would be different. Within days the incident went viral, protests breaking out across the country and, shortly thereafter, across the globe. Images of Floyd were even flashed from Syria, one of the world's most oppressed, war-torn countries, where young boys could be seen standing on a pile of rubble next to a large boulder painted with Floyd's image as a beacon of hope. On the stone was the writing "I can't breathe," as well as "No to Racism" (Porterfield, 2020). As the protests spread, several American cities became the focus of the civil rights protests. A few stand out for their unique responses to the Chauvin crime: Portland, Oregon, Seattle, Washington, and Washington, D.C.

Anti-police movements, both violent and nonviolent, rapidly spread. In Portland, Oregon, nonviolent anti-police demonstrations quickly became uncontained in the evening hours, with looting, fires, and the de-facing of government buildings becoming commonplace as the movement developed. In Seattle, Washington, police abandoned the downtown East Precinct after largely nonviolent protesters won their battle and developed a unique nonviolent community cooperative named the Capitol Hill Autonomous Zone, or "CHAZ." CHAZ, a territory bound by six city blocks, had its epicenter at the intersection of 12th and Pine Streets. CHAZ would be erected on June 8, 2020, and dismantled on July 1, 2020. Lastly, Washington, D.C. protests were snuffed by law enforcement's overly aggressive means of containing the predominantly negative nonviolent marchers. Indeed, Washington, D.C. shaped the shadow side of the zeitgeist.

The Trump administration, its policies, and President Trump himself were lightning rods for the upheaval building within the country. Many Americans felt trapped by the Trump presidency, his oppressive policies, misogyny, and racism imaged as the boot clamped firmly on the throats of many Americans. But it would be the murder of Floyd that would bring the truth to the surface, that racism remains unchanged in the architecture of the American soul. The enactment of the master-slave would further constellate the racial complex, making Floyd's murder *the* spark to set the fire. The Women's March and subsequent movements had primed the pump for explosive collective movement at hand. As protests began to form in Minneapolis, one could hear the drumbeat in the lines of Shelley's poem:

Rise like Lions after slumber
In unvanquishable number,
Shake your chains to earth like dew

Which in sleep had fallen on you -
Ye are many—they are few.

Indeed, the march is a collective signal that an adaptation crisis is at hand. The march provides the crucible in which violent communal forces can be catalyzed into new psychic life. This process begins within the individual and ends within the community, the march itself an orchestration of the collective's migratory instincts urging the herd into action. Through the march, members of the collective unconsciously link up and synchronistically come together in a collective movement defined by a similar purpose. Moreover, the march signals a disturbance in collective psychological, emotional, and spiritual well-being (Cunningham, 2020, p. 53).

Jungian analyst Thomas Singer writes extensively about cultural complexes and the inherent dangers within the spirit of groups that define the archetypal forces of the cultural complex. Similar to individual complexes, cultural complexes consist of affects, images, memories, and dreams that revolve around an archetypal core in the complex, defined by the culture within which it appears. In his article entitled "Unconscious Forces Shaping International Conflicts: Archetypal Defenses of the Group Spirit from Revolutionary America to Conflict in the Middle East" (2006), Singer states: "When this part of the collective psyche is activated, the most primitive psychological forces come alive for the purpose of defending the group and its collective spirit of Self" (p. 1). With the murder of Floyd, the values of the group were threatened on either side of the racist split. Blacks would point to the ongoing abuse of their civil liberties and the perpetuation of institutionalized racism, while the status quo resisted any change, accusing blacks and the "woke" (or the carriers of consciousness) of zealotry. Indeed, as if on cue, Americans began splitting off, choosing sides determined by one's color, ancestry, history, and the archetypal values of the group endemic in cultural complexes. The implementation of nonviolent protests demanded that the corrupt policing system be dismantled. It was the only way of dismembering the broken system. Still, it is as if no one realizes that the fix comes from within each individual protesting for change. Nevertheless, the reckoning for the work begins with a determination to find inner peace. This demand for justice began shaping the adaptive, emergent image of consciousness.

Nonviolent activism arises from the archetypal experience that is fundamental to individuation informing a spectrum of experience shaped by tactical, strategic principles on one end and philosophical, spiritual principles on another. Tactics, strategies, and tenets of nonviolence emerge through one's capacity to hold the tension of violence with a conscious intent to avoid harm to self and other. Nonviolence involves a conscious surrendering of aggression-laden, omnipotent defenses. The surrendering is a sacrifice of the ego in order to obtain a wider lens of experience, one which involves a connection to the greater good emerging from the Self.

Through the implementation of nonviolence, the complex began shifting as people were forced to face, once again, the problem of racism and oppression in America. The refusal to enact violence in the face of oppression and abuse induces suffering because the victims must tolerate their own pain in refusing retaliation. It is in the refusal to cause violence to another that the victim may experience their own capacity for compassion and mercy. They must also begin exploring what it means to be a victim left without redemption. And it is here that a surrender to something greater than oneself can emerge from the violent waters of envy and aggression.

Equally, the perpetrator is left with no one to fight but themselves. Thus, they must face their own aggressive tendencies. Brought together on the mutual field of suffering, nonviolence enforces reflection in both parties, thus momentarily disabling the projective mechanism, the projection only capable of producing repetition compulsions, fortifying the split within the complex and ensuring a calcification of aggression turned to hatred.

> Violence and nonviolence form a syzygy in nature itself its inextricable, serpentine flow informing the intrapsychic struggle, the dynamism from which the mythopoeic narrative of life emerges. Nonviolent activism is both an external and internal spiritual warfare. It is the sword-baring bearing feminine function of the psyche that cuts into unmediated aggression and violence, revealing the nonviolent potential for peace therein. The depth of this dynamic process is defined within the psyches of participants whose levels of self-related consciousness provide the vital nutrient for change.
>
> (Singer, 2021)

As the Civil Rights Movement demonstrated through nonviolent resistance, racism and the true nature of the racist could be split open, their interiority faced. Through nonviolent activism, people of color who suffered for hundreds of years at the hands of abuse aptly demonstrated how inner aggression and suffering can redeem one's sense of injustice. However, for nonviolence to penetrate violent psychic forces, one must be so sick of aggression, hatred, and violence that one is willing to die for peace. Nonviolence gives one access to the capacity to transform aggressive energy into love.

Turning once again to Shelly's *Mask of Anarchy*, archetypal nonviolence lends itself to the mystery of the soul's transformation. In the poem, archetypal nonviolent image manifests through the image of the feminine, in a figure called "Hope." Like Darnella Frazier, and Rosa Parks before her, she comes to deliver the nonviolent manifesto, ushered in on the wings of Mercurius:

Then she (hope) lay down in the street,
Right before the horses' feet,
Expecting, with a patient eye,
Murder, Fraud and Anarchy.

When between her and her foes
A mist, a light, an image rose,
Small at first, and weak, and frail
Like the vapour of a vale . . .

It grew—a Shape arrayed in mail
Brighter than the viper's scale,
And upborne on wings whose grain
Was as the light of sunny rain.
On its helm, seen far away,
A planet, like the Morning's lay;
And those plumes its light rained through
Like a shower of crimson dew.

With step as soft as wind it passed
O'er the heads of men—so fast
That they knew the presence there,
And looked,—but all was empty air.

As flowers beneath May's footstep waken,
As stars from Night's loose hair are shaken,

As waves arise when loud winds call,
Thoughts sprung where'er that step did fall.

Let a vast assembly be,
And with Great solemnity
Declare with measured words that ye
Are, as God has made ye, free-

Stand ye calm and resolute,
Lie a forest close and mute,
With folded arms and looks which are
Weapons of unvanquished war . . .

With folded arms and steady eyes,
And little fear, and less surprise,
Look upon them as they slay
Till their rage has died away.

Hope announces that freedom is a God-given right and that nonviolence is the spiritual weapon to be utilized against tyranny to regain and maintain that right.

As aptly demonstrated in the Chauvin case, nonviolent activism plays a critical role in the transformative powers of psychic libido. The George Floyd murder archetypally represents to the 2020 revolution what the Emmett murder in August 1955 was to the nonviolent Civil Rights movement. Like the racist enactments caught on camera in Montgomery bus boycotts, the Birmingham riots, and the marches in Selma, Eric Chauvin's depraved expression of ruthlessness staring into the camera, along with the image of his knee on Floyd's neck, awakened powerful memories of the collective trauma of slavery, its depravity, and the damage done to the American soul.

When Floyd was restrained and slowly dying, the racist split within the complex was activated by bipolar attractors, constellating in the group members an imperative to choose a side. A transgenerational wound re-opened, demanding reconciliation. Consequently, a shifting zeitgeist informed by a new consciousness was emerging through the Floyd protests. The protests represented a coming together of opposites, a *coniunctio* defined by the demand for a moral reconciliation for the injustices that African Americans and their ancestors had experienced for so long.

Cultural zeitgeists arise from collective adaptational shifts occurring through a cavalcade of internal and external psychic pressures impinging upon collective consciousness and its call for a new moral order. According to Steve McIntosh, in his book *Developmental Politics*:

> Moral systems are the products of collective agreements enforced through social norms, peer pressure, and the expectations of the larger community. And the effectiveness of these cultural agreements depends on a communitarian ethos—a binding sense of solidarity that emphasizes the sacrifice of the self for the sake of the larger group.
>
> (2020, p. 23)

This binding, systemic thrust is undergirded by the Self's tendency towards wholeness, determined by levels of consciousness within the zeitgeist.

Indeed, in cultural complexes, the individual psyches of the group who carry the transgenerational trauma and consciousness of the ancestors act as sparks of consciousness igniting the tip of the candle, the flame the attractor to like-minded individuals—a new image of freedom emerging once again, albeit in a different time and place. According to Nancy Kreiger, in her book *Bridges to Consciousness: Complexes and Complexity* (2013), consciousness emerges through the cavalcade of neuro-firings virally spreading: "The phase transition at a critical point transforms local into global functional connections which coordinate over widely dispersed functional and special areas. This synchrony over various functional areas is believed to lead to the experience of consciousness" (2013, p. 50). This description of individual consciousness can aptly serve as a metaphor for the similar spread of consciousness *en masse*.

Emblematically, Floyd's murder added another alchemical click in the wheel of unredeemed justice for the sufferers of America's racially violent history. The spread of protests indicated that something was coagulating within the unconscious in response to the one-sided cultural racist attitude. Indeed, Floyd's death and the collective's *coniunctio* had been coagulating in the collective unconscious for nearly sixty years (Civil Rights Movement). Outside of linear time and space, the complex constellates when the sulfuric heat of the collective unconscious finds an opening through the affectively loaded trauma within the complex. While many protests were violent, the nonviolent protests reaped the most interesting results, something tantamount to a collective psychic opening for peace emerging in the tension between violence and nonviolence. Such was the case in a small neighborhood in Seattle, Washington, called Capitol Hill and the creation of the Capitol Hill Autonomous Zone, or "CHAZ."

Washington state's West Coast was the shadow of the East Coast, Washington, D.C., the nation's capital. Seattle, a liberal city known for its highly educated, diverse, and progressive population, became the central focus of the protests after the Seattle police abandoned their precinct following violent confrontations with primarily peaceful protestors. Unlike Trump, Mayor Jenny Durkan supported the protestors' desire for peace and the establishment of an autonomous zone free from police oppression. Durkan was supported by the state's governor, Jay Inslee. Durkan and Inslee represented the positive archetypal anima and animus necessary for the emergence of the collective feminine germination called CHAZ in the face of Trump's oppressive tactics. CHAZ became one of many archetypal nonviolent images to emerge within the zeitgeist. CHAZ was a community cooperative and peace initiative designed to serve *all* members of the community. In the cultural complex of racism, CHAZ provided the collective dream image of equality and peace in a racially divided country. Once opened, CHAZ provided free goods, such as books, food, clothing, and free medical care. Nonviolent films and talks were central to discussions throughout the day, accompanied by music and dancing. In addition, a mandala-shaped community garden was established in Cal Anderson Park, just adjacent to the intersections of 12th and Pine Streets, the center of CHAZ.

Seen from above the city, the intersections of 12th and Pine form the image of the cross. The symbolism of the intersection is a sacred space where the archetypal forces of opposites meet, conducting an alchemical procedure of symbol formation. Symbolically, crossroads shape the union of opposites. This union of opposites produces an opening to a new way of being, but not without a struggle. According to the *Dictionary of Symbols*,

> Whatever the civilization, to reach the crossroads is to come face to face with the unknown. Since the natural human reaction to the unknown is one of fear, the primary aspect of the symbol is anxiety. In dreams, it betrays the wish for an important solemn and, in some sense, holy meeting. It may also show that a parting of the ways has been reached and that one must take a new and decisive direction of one's affairs. The symbolism of all traditions teaches that it seems to be necessary to pause at the

crossroads, as if a moment's thought, spiritual retreat, or even sacrifice has to be offered before setting off along a fresh path.

(p. 261)

In *Mysterium Coniunctionis*, Jung states: "The factors which come together in the *coniunctio* are conceived as opposites, either confronting one another in enmity or attracting one another in love" (Jung, 1970, para. 1). Jungian analyst and scholar Marie-Louise von Franz emphasizes this point when describing this alchemical union. "The *coniunctio* happens in the underworld, it happens in the dark when there is no light shining anymore. When you are completely out and consciousness is gone, then something is born or generated" (Von Franz, 1980, p. 162). Resonances of Shelley's *Mask of Anarchy* can be found in the image of hope preceding a force of nature rising up from the collective unconscious, providing the nonviolent intervention to change at the intersection between the known and the unknown, between death and new life. Indeed, hope shapes a particular kind of surrender to the forces of a conflict calcified by time.

Within the intersection of 12th and Pine, past and present collide as archetypal energies constellate. The nonviolent opening in the throes of violent protests announces the appearance of a third emergent phenomenon among opposites, the *coniunctio*, or an experience of psychological wholeness. CHAZ, a nonviolent autonomous zone free from police rule, emerges as a creative act engendered by the collective unconscious. The image of the Self appears through the number 12, symbolic of a life cycle ending, thus marking the beginning of a new life cycle (Chevalier et al., 1996, p. 1044). Pine Street, or the image of Pine, is symbolic of immortality, eternity, and fertility (Walker, 1988, p. 469). Moreover, the arrival of the circular community garden within CHAZ symbolizes a collective opening, a space of fertility, an archetypal font of creative energy. After establishing CHAZ, the organization "Black Lives Matter" would paint its slogan on Pine Street, the central image of the alchemical transformation collectively desired. The painting remains a permanent symbol of the uprisings in Seattle.

The reinstatement of local police led to a reckoning of CHAZ when the death of a 16-year-old boy called into question the protestor's capacity to protect themselves. The increase of violent outbreaks within and around CHAZ threatened its vital, lasting integrity. The community needed leadership and vision in order to maintain communal cohesion. Indeed, the alchemical vessel of CHAZ was perhaps too Utopian in concept, too fragile, without powerful forces to uphold its nonviolent ethos. This resulted in an alchemical *solutio* or de-construction of CHAZ. However, left behind was the residue of consciousness to be integrated by those in the collective who could carry it. Jungian analyst Edward Edinger (1995) discussed the importance of developing personal consciousness as an elixir for changing consciousness in the collective. For those in the CHAZ zone, holding a nonviolent stance within the context of violence allowed for the proliferation of consciousness through a *coniunctio*:

> You see, these individuals with insight into their own actions, who are aware of the operation of the opposites within themselves, have, to a greater or lesser extent, experienced the *coniunctio*—the subject matter of the *Mysterium*. Such people, then, are conscious carriers of the opposites. And, to the extent that such individuals exist and carry the opposites within themselves, they do not feed the exteriorization of the terrible strife between the opposites.
>
> (p. 325)

In Portland, Oregon, protestors rocked the ultra-liberal city with demands for equality for black Americans and other marginalized segments of society such as the LGBTQ contingent. The arrival of Shelley's hope emerged at the feet of police decked out in riot gear. Naked and sitting with legs wide open to the throngs of protestors and policemen, a female demonstrator, called "Naked Athena," announced her arrival (Image #4). Athena's image ushers in the archetypal fingerprint of nonviolence implemented in the throes of riots unique to Portland, her message as powerfully implemented as CHAZ was to Seattle. When asked why she had placed her naked body in front of a barrier of police officers, she stated that her sit-in happened entirely "off the cuff"—and felt "like being in the eye of the storm. . . . This fury arose in me . . . and I said I want to be naked, I want to confront them" (Lapine, 2020).

Athena is the patron goddess of heroic endeavor, the warrior goddess. In Portland, she is the nonviolent warrior goddess sitting between the protestors and the police mediating violence, the archetypal image arising organically through her aggression. Portland's Athena demonstrates the use of inner aggression as a nonviolent tincture to change. Indeed, to transmute violence or hatred, we need the presence of the other in order to induce a nonviolent activism within.

The projective psychic mechanisms that define the racist complex continue to cultivate the pathological splitting within America's political and social strata. In the 2020 Black Lives Matter movement, the national protests continued for weeks, abating momentarily with the deaths of John Lewis and C.T. Vivien, two giants in the Civil Rights Movement. Lewis' final crossing of the Edmond Pettus bridge served as a moment of silence on the battlefield, a reminder of nonviolence and existential power to induce reflection in the creation of the symbol.

The protests continue to enforce a collective reckoning. For those invested in maintaining a sense of power, their confessions have often been laced with sappy insincerity, inducing the firing of those who even vaguely smell like a racist. The sacrifices are self-serving. Yet other confessions have been conducted with compassion and education of the centuries-old white inflation and ignorance of the suffering of black Americans. According to Jung (1966), every analysis undergoes four stages of development: confession, elucidation, education, and transformation (CW16, par. 122). It seems that we are just beginning the process of confession with many citizens of all colors, unable to peel themselves away from the centuries-old projections of the rigidified master-slave relationship in racism. Indeed, the process of projective repeal is only in its infancy, stuck in the persona stage of development. The American ego has been shamed and guilted into change, its moral scaffolding shaky at best. Consequently, Americans flail in their capacities to be deeply reflective around race. Frightened of persecution, people have either shut down or been marginalized if they speak the truth of their racial bias or blindness.

In 2021, one year later, the protests drip on, the wisdom born of suffering in the black communities across America continually revising the narrative of the black American experience. The collective tension briefly abated with the election of the new president and the trial of Eric Chauvin ending with the verdict of guilty on second-degree unintentional murder, third-degree murder, and second-degree manslaughter. However, much of the 2020–2021 protest initiatives have led to a particular reckoning symbolically. As the marches in Selma led to passing of the Voting Rights Act of 1965, the Biden Administration has instituted the national Juneteenth holiday, marking the end of slavery. Moreover, educational institutions, organizations, and businesses have finally begun educational programs around race in America, a sad fact for 2021, since slavery came to America in 1619. These same programs are currently being contested across the country as well.

While these progressive movements seem to be trivial to many who have suffered under racism, it is the symbolic nodal point of consciousness which has emerged in the process that is important to acknowledge, for it bears psychic energy of consciousness and the redemption that is possible through a nonviolent way.

References

Chevalier, J., Gheerbrant, A., & Buchanan-Brown, J. (1996). *The Dictionary of Symbols*. London: Penguin Books.

Cunningham, R. M. (2020). *Archetypal Nonviolence King, Jung and Culture Through the Eyes of Selma*. London: Routledge.

Davies, J. E. (2011). Cultural Dimensions of Intersubjectivity. *Psychoanalytic Psychology*, 28(4), 549–559.

Edinger, E. (1995). *The Mysterium Lectures: A Journey Through C.G. Jung's Mysterium Coniunctionis*. Toronto, ON: Inner City Books.

Fairbairn, R. W. (1935/1994). The Sociological Significance of Communism Considered in the Light of Psycho-Analysis. *The British Journal of Medical Psychology*, 15(3), 218–229.

Gandhi, M. (1962). *The Essential Gandhi, an Anthology of His Writings on His Life, Work, and Ideas*. Edited by Louis Fischer. New York: Vintage Spiritual Classics.

Jung, C. (1966). *The Collected Works of C.G. Jung, Volume 16, the Practice of Psychotherapy*. Princeton, NJ: Princeton University Press.

Jung, C. (1970). *The Collected Works of C.G. Jung, Volume 14, Mysterium Coniunctionis*. Princeton, NJ: Princeton University Press.

Kurlansky, M. (2006). *Nonviolence the History of a Dangerous Idea*. New York, NY: Random House.

Lapine, T. (2020, July 27). *Portland Protester 'Naked Athena' Speaks Out: 'I am Notoriously Naked'*. Retrieved from https://nypost.com/2020/07/27/portland-protester-naked-athena-speaks-out-i-am-notoriously-naked/

McIntosh, S. (2020). *Developmental Politics*. St. Paul, MN: Paragon House Publications.

Montagnon, R. G. (2005). Do Be My Enemy for Friendship's Sake. *The Journal of Analytical Psychology*, 50(1), 27–34.

Nancy Kreiger, M. (2013). *Bridges to Consciousness: Complexes and Comlexity*. New York, NY and London: Routledge.

Pamela Power, E. B. (2014). "Negative Coniunctio" Envy and Sadomasochism in Analysis. In M. Winborn (Ed.), *Shared Realities*. Shaitook, OK: Fisher King Press.

Petri, F. (2014). Gandhi, Jung and Nonviolence Today. The Relevance of the Feminine in the Network Society. *India International Centre Quarterly*, 41(1), 7–18. http://www.jstor.org/stable/44733570

Porterfield, C. (2020, June 2). *Forbes.com/business*. Retrieved from www.forbes. com/sites/carlieporterfield/2020/06/02/street-artists-memorialize-george-floyd-worldwide-from-berlin-to-syria/?sh=1cbc9adf4035

Samuels, A. (1993). *The Political Psyche*. New York, NY: Routledge.

Shelley, P. B. (1932). *The Mask of Anarchy*. London: The Shelley Society's Publications.

Singer, T. (2006). Unconscious Forces Shaping International Conflicts: Archetypal Defenses of the Group Spirit from Revolutionary America to Confrontation in the Middle East. *The San Francisco Jung Institute Library Journal*, 25(4), 6–28. https://doi.org/10.1525/jung.1.2006.25.4.6

Singer, T. S. (2021). The March from Selma to Montgomery and the Nonviolent Movement in Analysis. In M. Renee and M. Cunningham (Eds.), *The Reality of Fragmentation and the Yearning for Healing: Jungian Perspectives on Democracy, Power and Illusion in Contemporary Politics*. An Online Book. San Francisco: ARAS Publications.

Von Franz, M.-L. (1980). *Alchemy An Introduction to the Symbolism and the Psychology*. Toronto, ON: Inner City Books.

Von Franz, M.-L. (1995). *Projection and Re-Collection in Jungian Psychology*. London: Open Court Press.

Walker, B. G. (1988). *The Women's Dictionary Symbols and Sacred Objects*. San Francisco, CA: Harper Collins.

Wikipedia. (2023a, November 24). Buddhism. *Wikipedia, the Free Encyclopedia*. Retrieved from https://en.wikipedia.org/w/index.php?title=Buddhism& oldid=1186664662

Wikipedia. (2023b, November 30). Satyagraha. *Wikipedia, the Free Encyclopedia*. Retrieved from https://en.wikipedia.org/w/index.php?title=Satyagraha& oldid=1187588463

Wirtz, U. (2021). *Trauma and Beyond*. New York, NY and London: Routledge.

Chapter 3

The Dark Feminine Rising
A Psychocultural and Clinical Meditation

Ronnie Landau

The Ancient One That Is She

According to some scholars, a beautiful set of early gnostic manuscripts called the *Nag Hammadi* were discovered in 1945. They were translated from Greek into Coptic and said to be originally written between the second and fourth century AD. One portion of these translated texts called *The Thunder, Perfect Mind* expresses the ancient archetypal dimension of the dark feminine. "She" is referred to as the first and last and the honored and scorned, both holy and a whore. "She" exemplifies modesty and boldness and is both shameless and ashamed. Holding the tension of the opposites, she is spoken of as modesty and boldness, strength and fear. She embodies the qualities of joining and dissolving and her voice cries out to be heard with reverence as she manifests elements of a feminine wisdom that has been banished. In considering that the ancient one that is *she* is an aspect of the psyche calling out, rising from the depths of our essential being, "she" is need of integration. It may be a matter of survival as we face the current dire elements challenging our human existence.

In the Womb of the Dark Feminine

This reflection on the dark feminine in culture and Jungian clinical practice is partly a response to a world that feels increasingly more frightening, "on fire," in its rapidly escalating chaos, suffering, and turmoil. The current global ethos is contributing to levels of psychological angst both individually and collectively. In its more extreme and dire manifestations, it raises questions as to the sustainability of our humanity. To this point, I am keenly aware of the extent to which *the dark feminine* is a significant dynamism in the current Zeitgeist.

DOI: 10.4324/9781003252993-4

As ongoing fears of volatility, vulnerability, and uncertainty arise and seep into our personal and cultural perspectives, we find ourselves having to face a kind of psychic groundlessness. Within this state of groundlessness, an opportunity roams albeit instinctive in nature, to engage in a dialogue with the looming inner darkness rather than avoid it or deny our distress. The process of dialogue with inner darkness requires a full engagement with our feeling life, our affects, our emotions in order to actualize aspects of selfhood that have been exiled. "Where there is no emotion there is no life . . . the fire has to burn the fire, one just has to burn in the emotion till the fire dies down and becomes balanced" (Von Franz, 1980, p. 252). The alchemical process of *calcinatio* or the heating up of emotion must be endured for redemption and transformation. Simply stated, the experience of the dark archetypal feminine rising will generate a wide range of emotional states, *I feel, therefore I am.*

Ancestral Tracking

What we are only now beginning to become conscious of is the side of the feminine archetype that cannot, nor does it even necessarily desire to, fit into the existing cultural structures. That other side has best been described as the Dark Feminine.

(Gustafson, 2003a)

The presence of dark feminine energy in culture worldwide continues in its unconscious fury because it has been largely reviled and ignored for over 3,000 years. Jungian analyst Betty De Shong Meador offers, "During the 3,000 years of conscious dominance in the Western world of the masculine god, a concomitantly powerful feminine presence has been building in the unconscious" (Meador, 1994, p. 32). In *Uncursing the Dark, Treasures from the Underworld*, Meador states, "We must correct the phallic definition of women prevalent in our culture, a definition that requires women to suppress or devalue their own female nature" (1994, p. 127). Meador amplifies the needed re-emergence of the archetypal feminine in its darker forms through a brief analysis of author Doris Lessing's dystopian novel *Memoirs of a Survivor*, published in 1974. She describes this novel as an example of "how the rule of patriarchy which has held civilization together will come down" (1994, p. 34). Now that patriarchal structures in Western culture are more consistently being challenged, the dark feminine is being "known again" but not always welcomed. It continues to threaten embedded cultural structures in ways that can still feel apocalyptic in nature. Perhaps the apocalyptic aspect of deep change is what is needed, and Lessing got it right.

Although it can be said that "patriarchal rigidity is crumbling throughout the world," there are continued efforts in the form of regressive attempts to restore the hegemony of the Father in every possible fashion—social, cultural, religious" (Stein, 2003, preface). An active engagement with the dark feminine is essential in order to bring about real change and transformation worldwide. Efforts to make space for personal transformation requires the analyst to set aside cultural biases and attend to the unconscious with great humility in the hopes of facilitating a shift in consciousness to "uncurse the dark" (Meador, 1994).

As Jungian analysts, we are mentored to become highly attuned to the unconscious movements of psyche, both personal and collective. Jung writes about the multitude of ways that psychological content that has been defensively repressed will reside in what he calls *shadow* and, ultimately, will likely surface in symbolic images. Jung references shadow as a "moral problem that challenges the whole ego-personality" (CW 9i, par. 14). In considering the moral challenge of encountering shadow as Jung describes it by assigning it to the individual ego, one can easily make the leap to query about its relevance on a collective level. Jung suggests we start with ourselves; we must look into our dark places and spaces, while also maintaining a connection to the world around us. When we risk looking into the fire of the womb of the archetypal dark feminine, we might become frightened by what we see, the shadowy realms of our own nature.

Jungian analytic practice often involves a process of symbolically tracking unconscious footprints of what is manifesting somatically and psychologically with our analysands. It includes exploring the terrain of painful personal histories and complex ancestral backgrounds. The emphasis of analytic work most often requires a conscious holding of tensions, multiplicities, opposites, and difference. The willingness to engage with psychological complexity, individual and collective, can be viewed as a kind of moral and ethical commitment implicit in the process of doing Jungian analysis, as I see and experience it. Additionally, the task of holding one's attention to experiences of the individual as well as the larger world is profoundly challenging. It beckons us to ground ourselves in an attitude of respect for the unknown and patience with uncertainty.

In metaphoric conversations with the unconscious psyche, we may find our-selves encountering terrifying beasts, apocalyptic tsunamis, and dry, burned-out, abandoned landscapes while roaming expansive forests, diving into the vastness of dark oceans, or learning to speak "whale," as one of my analy-sands referenced. The journeys are mysterious and humbling as we commit ourselves to remaining still, observing, and honoring a vow of silence when needed, in order to meet the grace and wisdom that comes with the endur-ing acceptance of facing the complexities of the human spirit. To reflect and hold the tension of inner and outer worlds continues to call upon a process of what Jung called *lunar consciousness*. Lunar consciousness, the psycho-logical equivalent to Eros for Jung, is a function of the primordial archetypal feminine principle, and it embodies qualities of creativity, instinctuality, and intuition. When such a function goes underground, the world grows darker, more one-sided and polarized, and, ultimately, more dangerous.

Jung and Encounters With the Dark Feminine

Historically speaking, Jung himself experienced significant concerns in response to the patterns manifesting in the culture and collective psyche of his time. His own confrontation with aspects of his painful inner life chal-lenges began in November of 1913. According to Jung, the movement into his own darkness was the result of devastating disappointments in response to his rupture with Freud. Jung's level of psychic disintegration that took the form of disturbing fantasies was likely exacerbated by his deep concerns about the culture at large and about what ultimately became the eruption of WW1. These highly significant events in his life have become widely known as "Jung's descent into the underworld, in search of his lost soul." Jung began to record his fantasies in the *Black Books* and his writings and drawings creatively culminated in the opus of the *Red Book or Liber Novus*. It is interesting to note that while Jung wrote the *Red Book* in the modern era, it was not published until 2009, coinciding with the deconstructing and chaotic movements that began to unfold in post-modernity, the timing perhaps synchronistic and worthy of notation (Furlotti, 2017). Jung's spe-cific encounters with aspects of the archetypal dark feminine manifested in active imaginations with a figure he called Salome, his *anima*. Although Jung's outer world was troubling as ours is today, the specific circumstances of his inherited cultural and social conditions are vastly different. Through Jung's attentiveness to this dark period in his own inner suffering as well as his capacity to look beyond himself, he discovered a working framework, what he called *the spirit of the times and the spirit of the depths*. In considering Jung's notion of the "spirit of the times and the spirit of the depths," we might also imagine the degree to which individual trauma and collective trauma are inescapably intertwined in overlapping dynamics, moment by moment, whether we are aware of it or not. What we now call "transgenerational" or "intergenerational trauma" helps to inform our psychological understanding of the intersection of the individual personality with larger historical and cultural influences. The significance of the dark feminine is a point of entry into understanding aspects of trauma, both individual and collective. In Fred Gustafson's poignant and timely book *The Moonlit Path: Reflections of the Dark Feminine*, he states,

> We now live in a time when manifestations of the archetypal feminine confront us at every turn. Reconsiderations in how we educate, how we do economics, how we use the environment, do our politics, conduct business, live and die are all being challenged. What we mean by the Dark Feminine is playing a major role behind all of them. In the last analysis, each individual will have to answer for him or herself how the missing feminine is trying to be played out in his or her life.
>
> (2003b, p. xvii)

Making the unconscious conscious is a well-known *dictum* in Jungian thought: it is essentially the theoretical bedrock of analysis that facilitates healing, growth, and maturation. Following this dictum, Jung informs us that what is not made conscious in our lives inevitably falls into the unconscious aspect of our human existence and will be experienced ultimately as our fate, *or "fatum"* (Latin, meaning "what has been destined"). "The psychological rule says that when an inner situation is not made conscious, it happens outside as fate" (CW9ii, par. 126). To further amplify this dynamic, according to Greek and Roman mythology, the three Fates or Moirai, were Goddesses who presided over the lifespan of all humanity. They were known as Clotho, Lachesis, and Atropos, a kind of divine feminine power that held the mysterious tapestry of existence in their hands. Clotho, Lachesis, and Atropos were once seen as the weavers of the mother threads of life and death. As the myth goes, Clotho spun the threads of life, Lachesis measured the thread allotted to each person, and Atropos was the discerning cutter who severed the red thread, thus determining our ultimate passing. The mythological manifestation of the three Fates is a metaphorical example of how the powerful karmic-like energies of life and death were once held by aspects of the archetypal feminine. From such origins, we can imagine how the archetypal feminine holds within her grip both the dark and light aspects of life itself and the temporality of what it is to be human. This is but one mythopoetic example of how the archetypal feminine was viewed as the keeper of the mysteries of life and death.

The power of the feminine throughout history and culture has been eroded and denigrated under the potent and persistent infusion of patriarchal values. Psychic content, be it personal or collective, that gets maligned, ignored, and/or dissociated will return; this a basic tenet of Jung's theory of the personal and archetypal unconscious and *the return of the repressed*. One might muse for the sake of this chapter that the volume of repressed feminine qualities that have been pathologically ignored under the weight of patriarchal structures has contributed to a *darker than dark*, or *blacker than black*, aspect of the archetypal feminine, whose affective expression is rage. Where and how does the dark feminine begin to express its fury in response to being ignored? According to Jung, symbolic manifestations of disavowed and repressed psychic content that have been buried in shadow are revealed in powerful affectively charged expressions or feeling states and complexes. When the affective and feeling channels of our humanity are defensively blocked, they may take various forms of psychic dis-ease in the form of depression or anxiety or lodge themselves in the body as physical symptoms or serious illness, such as Bessel van der Kolk, M.D. describes in his book *The Body Keeps the Score* (2015).

Dreams additionally provide powerful compensatory activity which bring to consciousness aspects of shadow in need of integration. Recently, I was privileged to hear a brief dream of a new analysand. She described being in a garden where she saw herself; rather there were two of her. She recognized one figure as herself, and the other was quite dark and frightening. As she moved towards herself, the darker woman bit her. The dark feminine had made herself known, without much in the way of symbolic disguises; it was undeniably a part of herself. As psychoanalysts in clinical practice, we understand how often our personal wounds and the challenges of our pursuing individuation can and will intersect with those of our analysands. We often consider such phenomena as synchronicities at work, in concert with the dynamic engineering of the Self. Her most recent dream was telling, affirming, and deeply meaningful to both of us in providing a doorway into the dark archetypal feminine as "feminine instinctuality in the culture often lives in unsavory places" (Meador, 1994, p. 54).

Queens and Hairy Legs

My encounters with the dark side of the archetypal feminine took fuller expression almost two decades ago while finishing my thesis for becoming a Jungian analyst. During this process, I was rivetted by the discovery of a rather simple quote from Jung where he refers to the "loss of an archetype" as that which "gives rise to that frightening discontent in our culture" (Vol 9i). Jung's linking the loss of an archetype in culture to the notion of collective trauma, as I interpreted his quote, served as further affirmation of my thesis hypothesis and topic, "The Queen of Sheba and Her Hairy Legs: The Redemption of the Exiled Erotic Feminine in Western Monotheism and Jungian Analytic Practice."

The process of writing the thesis was itself a psychological descent, but as my body entered the process, I was forced to acknowledge even deeper levels of neglect of the dark feminine in my psyche. I developed thyroid cancer while conducting my research, a mysterious lump appearing on my throat chakra as my legs grew hairy. My thyroid cancer coincided and further served as confirmation of my needing to find my own authentic voice devoid of the remnants of powerful patriarchal influences (patriarchy meaning literally "rule of the father"). I had unconsciously banished a level of my own feminine nature from my psyche, and "since we all grow up in a society with patriarchal values, we find the archetypal feminine primarily in the unconscious," (Meador, 1994, p. 146) separate from the influence of culturally driven expectations and limitations.

Like many women in my generation, confronting the wounded aspects of my patriarchally infused upbringing has been challenging. In her book *Jung: A Feminist Revision*, Susan Rowland comments, "Patriarchal ideology depends upon the suppression of the feminine as inferiority" (2002, p. 7). This resonates deeply with my own experience both personally and collectively. As I enter my *crone* years, the aging process contributes to yet another layer of confrontation of what it means to be a woman, an older woman, and how the *aging feminine* is viewed, experienced, and lived in the collective. The work of redeeming shadow aspects of the dark feminine continues to burn in my cronehood years. Sometimes it flickers rather softly like moonlight, and other times its raging feminine heat provides the energy to foster deep change and the necessary courage to write frankly and openly on this subject.

The Lilith Effect: The Return of the Repressed

The following passages read rather like an active imagination (a method of assimilating unconscious contents) as well an attempt at a form of feminine writing. Its origins arose from an inner call to speak directly from the fiery archetypal feminine perspective on the erotic with a specific focus on the subject of rage. Psychologically speaking, a disconnection from aspects of the erotic feminine lives throughout humankind, whether men, women, gay, lesbian, queer, transgender, and gender non-binary individuals, because this disconnection is archetypal. It is often in its darkness that it makes itself known. As the influx of greater acceptance of gender fluidity exists, more questions and dialogues evolve as to what is meant by genderized notions of masculine and feminine. The search for connection to the dark feminine continues to burn in the psyches of many as we struggle to recover what has been dissociated and maligned. It is both a personal and a culturally collective demand.

Lilith Insists on Speaking First

Here are a few verses from the American poet Pamela Hadas from her book of poetry titled *The Passion of Lilith* (1976, p. 4).

> What had the likes of me
> To do with Adam?
> Yet, by after-whim or black with humor of Him
> We were thrown together, clay seen and glaze of moon . . .
> Then Adam nearly drove me mad—my original gaping letter-man,
> docile as a stamp
> And bland as logic –
> Flapping forever the divine right of his real estate.
> At my obvious lack of properties.
> He wouldn't lie under my crazy quilts or improvise.
> He'd rather die.

The incubation of my thoughts about feminine rage and its transformative potential has necessitated a long dark gestational process. This incubation has at times been filled with fear, doubt, and guilt, as to whether anything was to be born in this post-menopausal body and psyche. One hears in this reflection of doubt the remnants of a patriarchal inner structure projecting itself onto a creative process, not an uncommon experience for me and not particularly welcomed as you might imagine.

A creative approach to the topic of feminine rage and the redemption of the erotic could only be engaged through my willingness to surrender and submerge myself once again into the depths of a feminine principle, honoring its mysterious, non-linear, chaotic, and non-rational parts. This psychic landscape remains uncomfortable and manifests in my body like a huge weight on my chest and pressure in my groin. I feel the familiar resistance to succumb to the below-ness of it, like plunging beneath a wave into the vastness of the ocean, holding my breath as I go under.

While struggling with *what is to be said*, and *who will speak* about feminine rage and its connection to erotic life, I considered that this gestation was inchoate. By this I mean psychically inherited before I was born, the first child, a female, to first-generation Jewish immigrant parents from Poland. The patriarchal silencing of the feminine voice was pre-immanent, epigenetically speaking, woven into the fabric of my "psychic" DNA long before I appeared. The shadow of my patriarchal inheritance, born partly out of a religious immigrant Jewish family, remained safely unconscious in my psyche. It was psychologically sealed off and encapsulated in my "neurotic" adaptations as a father's dutiful daughter, devoid of many aspects of my own feminine imagination and instinctual nature.

Regarding the archetype, Jung tells us that it "might be suitably described as the instinct's perception of itself or as the self portrait of the instinct" (1972, para 277). As Jungians, when we speak about the archetypal realm, we are referencing the intimate connection between instinct and its inborn potentials. The instinctual realm necessitates the interaction of soma/body and psyche. Early, when Jung was distinguishing his theory from Freud's emphasis on a biological drive-oriented psychology, he eventually found himself strongly pulled towards the *numinous*, the spiritual quest, the heroic journey, and transcendence, leaving behind aspects of the primal, embodied, semiotic elements of our nature, in particular the feminine essence that resides in the darkness, the wetness, the earth, and the birthing process. Jung's focus of interest regarding the *feminine principle* and *femininity* was primarily consumed by the mysterious qualities of the anima, an eternal manifestation of the feminine soul in the masculine. His views on the anima were strongly influenced by his own personal experiences of his mother, his wife, and his muses, real and imagined. Jung tells us, "Woman, with her very dissimilar psychology, is and always has been a source of information about things for which a man has no eyes." (CW 7, 186)

Freud characterized feminine sexuality as the *dark continent* of psychoanalysis. Stated simply, his phallocentric perspective on femininity was that women were born little men, found themselves lacking, and *became* filled with penis envy. The impact of Freudian theory highlights the notion that women are lacking in relation to men. Jung, in departing from Freud's notion of femaleness, turned toward the construct of the *feminine principle*, equating it with Eros, feeling, receptivity, and relatedness. The masculine, for Jung, was designated as Logos, an active principle, the thinking function. Jung's binary design, when concretized, suggests that women feel and relate, and men think. This classical tenet in Jungian theory, when explored through the lens of gender, is constricting to both femaleness and maleness. It is challenging to tease apart the *massa confuse* of gender and culture from archetypal manifestations and symbolic language. "The framework of culture has such a binding effect that nature's instinctual pull can be held in bondage to the consensual perceptions and beliefs of a society" (Meador, 1994, p. 116).

In Jungian parlance, when some aspect of our nature has been dissociated, it will build up intense and powerful compensatory energy in the unconscious, Jung's notion of one-sidedness and the interplay of opposites. What is denied consciously will intensify in the unconscious, Jung's concept of "shadow" with its archetypal roots.

One aspect of the voice of feminine rage is in direct response to the oppression and devaluation of what I'm calling the darker feminine qualities in our nature, inclusive of the erotic, sensual, and sexual. Beneath a vast blanket of collective adaptation, centuries old, lies the transgressive anger, the fiery rage, and unrelenting wrath of a powerful unlived archetypal energy trying to find expression now more than ever. When we dare to look directly into the face of feminine rage, we are reminded of Freud's question—*what do women want*? For Jungians, the question might be, *what does the feminine want?* Equality, status, respect, justice, power, apology, revenge. It is difficult to find the words to satisfy the impassioned calling from the depths where the core of feminine rage resides. When I listen more deeply, ear to the ground, attending to what needs to be said, I hear only howling, wailing, sobbing, and screeching. This has remained a wordless place. The repressed primal archetypal feminine and her terrifying power waits in the darkness to compel women to re-engage with their own nature.

It was not until entering Jungian analytic training that traces of my own archetypal inheritance of the split-off dark feminine became disorienting as well as fodder for my individuation. But the element of rage, my rage, initially remained deeply buried. Occasionally it made a somatic appearance in the form of migraine headaches which began in my adolescent years. I did not know or understand over 25 years ago what I'm now calling the *Lilith effect*, the *return of the repressed*, a particular form of dissociation in response to marginalized aspects of femaleness and the feminine soul. The *Lilith effect* is not exclusive to women, however; straight, gay, queer, lesbian, and transgender individuals are vulnerable to this form of dissociation as we all share the complexity of cultural, biological, and psychological responses to *the power of the feminine*.

In this brief personal narrative, I found initial support and comfort in Jung's notion that any theory of psychology is also a *subjective confession*. However, embracing this well-known Jungian tenet did not insulate me from feeling that my opening stance was indulgent and risky. To cloak my position in well-curated theory would have been a far safer methodology to expand on this subject matter. Unbidden, I was confronted by my own patriarchal attitudes as questions arose in my mind as to what would be heard and viewed as sound intellectual property worthy of listening to and thinking about. A rebellious voice from the outcasted part of my feminine identity arose. Just stop!

If I'm willing to be faithful to the topic of feminine rage and its capacity to redeem the darker archetypal aspects of the feminine inclusive of the erotic, I must speak fully through and from my experience, from the core of my sense of being a woman, and the type of woman I know myself to be. I was reminded of Esther Harding's wisdom in her book *Women's Mysteries* where she says that a woman needs to be true to her own nature and not contract for individuation to occur.

The alchemy of this writing project brought me back to the threshold of a more-than-20-year-old memory I'm calling *the case of the red lips*. The case of the red lips refers to my unapologetic refusal to change or subdue my red lipstick colour, Red Lizard, while in Jungian analytic training. While this was certainly not a verbalized requirement, it was an unusual phenomenon amidst my training ethos. I often imagined the murmuring behind closed doors while walking into or out of classes and supervisions.

At times I reflected on my narcissistic needs to be seen. I was surprised to discover that my female colleagues, mentors, and supervisors often had reactions to my red lips. I experienced their quiet commentaries as a mixture of fear, envy, and concern for me. Hidden in the tincture of their message was the hushed tone of a patriarchal attitude.

As I recall the nature of this ultimately individuating experience, I realize my inner Lilith was outing herself. She was unwilling to submit, refusing to heed and obey the cautionary warnings from my sisters, who, like a Greek chorus, whispered, "Be careful, don't be too much, too visible, to bold, too sensual." Upon reflection, I'm somewhat stunned that nothing back then could persuade me from my Red Lizard lips, not even the fear and risk of tainting my reputation as a serious-minded Jungian training candidate.

Patriarchy lives in men and women, let's be clear. Psychological patriarchy aligns and identifies with the idea of male dominance and power. Women have been strongly influenced and profoundly wounded by unconscious patriarchy often through the mother-line. The mother-daughter relationship carries the weight and legacy of transgenerational trauma that women embody in response to a male-dominated culture. What's a mother to do?

This description matches perfectly with my own psychological inheritance and maternal experience of being raised by a mother, a dutiful wife, a "woman of valor," who found herself imprisoned in a patriarchal structure, inner and outer. Her unconscious primal rage took the form of a mild but persistent chronic depression that occasionally manifested in crippling mouth sores, leaving her unable to speak or eat food that required biting and chewing.

The psychological awareness of the power of this transgenerational wounding from mothers to daughters broke open while writing this paper. I was flooded with grief as the carefully crafted walls of protection around my mother, her mother, and so forth shattered. The wounding of patriarchy in women reveals itself in our consulting rooms when the suffering becomes too great. Often the masculine-like scaffolding begins to crumble as the fragile sense of feminine self can no longer hold the centre. For such a woman, it becomes a battle between life and death, the *Lilith effect* so existentially terrifying that

> adaptation to the culture imposes on most women a masculine-orienting frame which gives life meaning and predictability. The frame serves

to guide her outer life in the absence of the development of consciousness of the feminine in her formative years. She becomes a phallus with breasts. The masculine frame is built over a lack, the absence of the feminine. She is terrified when this frame begins to fall away, for she senses the underlying void.

(Meador, p. 152)

A female analysand, a victim of early-childhood abuse, was trying to recover the exiled feminine parts of her psyche. The transgenerational trauma and shame of her Native American ancestral origins contributed to further banishment of essential aspects of her nature as her well-crafted professional persona hid the authentic aspects and beauty of her natural being. In her characteristically frozen style, utterly void of affect, she shared what I knew to be a deeply painful memory. At the budding age of 21, she asked her mother to assist her in getting a total hysterectomy. Her competitive masculinized edge exacerbated her fear that her monthly menstrual cycle would interfere in her studies in medical school at Harvard University. For my analysand, being a woman represented a state of inferiority— physiologically and psychologically—that she desperately wanted to amputate. Approaching the age of 40, she sought out Jungian analysis in response to a disturbing but numinous dream, in addition to being well read in philosophy and psychoanalysis. This brilliant, accomplished woman resided in a cold, barren wasteland. Her capacity for healthy relationality, Eros, sexuality, and creativity, severed by early trauma and neglect, left her imprisoned in a crippling compensatory inner patriarchy and toxic self-hatred. It manifested in an overidentification with Logos and intellect, mentalizing being her method of meeting the outer world where she could imagine herself to be more a man than the men she knew. She rejoiced in deep satisfaction over the domination and power she felt while remaining dissociated from her own body and from her potential for relatedness.

Demaris Wehr, in *Jung and Feminism*, writes about the "self-hater" in women. "Internalized oppression feels a certain way inside a woman, it speaks with a certain voice, and it has a certain effect on her" (1987, p. 18). The experience of my analysand's erupting rage was terrifying to her. She feared it would destroy her and annihilate her professional career. She eventually dropped out of treatment to work abroad, having been offered a much-desired promotion. The need to triumph professionally and remain encapsulated in her complex prevailed. While I had felt we were a good fit and had co-created a safe-enough analytic container, her fear, ambivalence, and resistance towards change was pronounced.

As many of us know, we are talking about the capacity to allow for a psychological process of de-integration, a coming apart in order to rebirth ourselves. The ego needs to feel and be strong enough to tolerate the psychic disintegration, the falling apart of inner structures that are no longer adaptive or healthy to one's well-being.

Recently, the pandemic brought her back to her home turf, and she reached out to meet virtually. She re-entered in a state of despair and psychic dismemberment. She had been drawn into the dark underworld of a highly volatile and abusive relationship where her life was seriously endangered. Broken apart by the torture and shame of her brief dysfunctional marriage, she recognized the degree to which her life depended on coming to terms with the amputated parts of her instinctual life. Her rage returned, then gradually softened into profound grief for the young innocent parts of herself that had gone into hiding.

As the masculine false-self scaffolding melted from the heat of her grief, she dreamt of a feral waif-like young girl hiding in an underground tunnel. She dreamt of an apocalyptic landscape—a dry, dusty red clay-like desert, a dystopian image of the *Mad Max* genre, where she discovered herself growing new arms and hands that attached at her shoulder like a Handless Maiden. Her story is many women's story; it is unique and collective, deeply private, and archetypal. But feminine rage is not confined to women.

A male analysand who was in great conflict with his erotic and sexual instinctual life due to religious teachings during his childhood became enraged with me and took pleasure informing me that his negative transference was classically Kleinian, not Jungian. I was "the bad-breast witch." After holding and tolerating his deep emotional pain expressed in the form of verbal assaults, and in threats to fire me and replace me with a good Freudian male analyst, he confessed that it often felt to him like the heat of his anger was feminine in nature. It was a deeply softening and touching moment for both of us as he began to reconnect to an essential aspect of his *being*. Psychoanalyst Harry Guntrip, in discussing repression, withdrawal, and dissociation, says that it is always the female element that we find dissociated in both men and women. The ruthless capacity on the part of the analyst to tolerate the primal searing rage of a wounded feminine element necessitates being *capable* of holding safe space for the recovery of heathy instinct, particularly of the erotic. To do so means that the analyst themselves have encountered enough of their own primal rage. It is the essential ingredient needed to get well and goes beyond one's capacity to be therapeutically supportive.

The *Lilith effect* is the consequence of over 3,000 years of a patriarchally driven culture that fears the feminine instinctual element, banishing all that is dark, ugly, shameful, violent, autonomous, and sensual. According to Judaic myth, Lilith was vile, a demon, a hag, a succubus, and a witch. Based on this description, she is nothing you long to become or want to come home to. The name "Lilith" in Hebrew translates as "night monster." In ancient times and even today, amulets are used to ward off Lilith's fearsome psychopathic-like rage. Lilith is said to kill newborn infants and steal men's semen while they are asleep, a likely justification for nocturnal emissions. Lilith's importance to the psychology of women and the archetype of the feminine in general is highlighted in D. McNeely's brilliant book *Mercury Rising: Women, Evil and the Trickster Gods*. She speaks of Lilith's rage as being "born out of her failure to be recognized in her authenticity," and she notes that Lilith is the part of the Great Goddess that has been rejected, qualities of the feminine self that the Shekina alone does not carry, particularly instinctuality and sexuality (McNeely, 1996, p. 132).

Lilith carries between her legs the fiery rage of the scorned feminine element. She represents a kind of feminine power akin to what the French feminist psychoanalyst Luce Irigaray describes as "an insatiable hunger, a voracity of desire, that swallows you whole" (Irigaray, 1997, p. 29).

Luce Irigaray, Julia Kristeva, and other feminist psychoanalysts search in their writings for feminine psychoanalytic language, imagination, and theory. One way to consider their contributions is as a movement to shift what has been a rather one-sided and predominantly masculine and patriarchal-oriented theoretical foundation where women suffer from Freud's penis envy and Jung's animus possession.

She Who Does Not Obey—the Rage-Filled Return of the Repressed

"Holding the image of Lilith's fire offers insight into the overwhelming rage, which has yet to be explored . . . she is the fire and the rage against diminishment" (Kamerling, 2003, p. 109). Jewish *midrashic* literature written in the thirteenth century tells us that Lilith was Adam's first wife. God created Adam, man, and Lilith, woman, equally, at the exact same time, from the clay of the earth. This stands in sharp contrast to the Genesis telling where God made Eve *for man* from Adam's rib. Lilith has been known as "the one who engendered Adam's soul," for he had no soul until then. She was the very first woman who tasted the forbidden fruit from the tree of knowledge and found out that "desire is sweet." Possessing this knowledge, she begins to argue with Adam and refuses to lie underneath him during sexual intercourse. While quarreling with Adam, Lilith commits a sin: she says God's name aloud and flies into the air to reside in a cave, in the desert, off the Red Sea.

Adam, dejected, enlists Gods help, whereupon God sends three angels to bring back Lilith. She refuses to return and, as a consequence of her disobedience, is cursed by God with the fate of giving birth to one hundred demons daily. God then went on to create Eve, a better and less problematic version of woman, or so it seemed. Lilith's place of exile and desolation has been described in the Old Testament as a wasteland drenched with blood, the haunt of pelicans, owls, and ravens. Jewish historian and anthropologist Raphael Patai informs us the letters of her name add up to *screech. Lilith* is called the demon of screeching (Patai, 1990).

Lilith and the Queen of Sheba share skin. It has been noted that the beautiful exotic queen who visited King Solomon was in fact Lilith. According to Jewish legend, the riddles that Sheba posed to Solomon are a repetition of the words of seduction that Lilith used on Adam. Lilith was, in some cultures, considered to be dark skinned and/or goat footed, again a kind of misogynist viewing of the instinctual feminine as shameful, inferior, and demonic. Lilith is associated with the serpent in the Garden of Eden. She embodies the darkest fear men have of women, their bodies, and female sexuality. It is the Lilith/Eve conflation that has been used to identify women as the true source of evil in the world.

I had a brief and compelling dream, an image of myself while writing this passage. On my right shoulder a patch of black feathers were growing. In disbelief I wondered, was this my body, was it a disease, was it permanent? I pulled at it firmly and realized I could remove this strange bodily mutation of black feathers. I felt some relief in knowing I had partial autonomy over this mysterious manifestation. When I awoke, dismissing the idea of an impending Aronofsky *Black Swan* psychosis, I immediately thought about Lilith and her connection to owls and ravens. I recognized the depth to which contact with this archetypal energy was taking form on me and in me. Something instinctual, non-human, and shamanic in nature had been revealed.

This dream served to facilitate my understanding of the shamanic trickster-like aspect of Lilith's archetypal landscape. As the raven is the great messenger, and the owl a form of wisdom that sees in the darkest of places, so it is with Lilith in her shape-shifting aspect of dark, erotic, instinctual feminine. She is a symbolic manifestation of an essentially creative, transformative element guided by the Self. Lilith, the mercurial feminine, the animating natural level of being, will not be tamed, tampered with, or domesticated.

The renewal of interest in Lilith is testimony to a rebirth in human consciousness. "The myth of Lilith suggests a way to break the fixation with 'being below, repressed and maltreated'" (Colonna, 1980). I would offer that the breaking of this fixation is needed not only for women but for all those that suffer the affliction of oppression worldwide. What we heal in ourselves, we heal in the world, as implied by Jung's notion of the *Unus Mundus*. Poetry often gives us access to aspects of ourselves that other forms of narration may not be able to express. The African American memoirist, civil rights activist, and poet Maya Angelou (1928–2014), in her poem *Still I Rise*, written in 1976, offers us a deeply affective reflection of need to break the binds of oppression. The following are a few of her powerful words from this poem.

You may write me down in history
With your bitter twisted lies,
You may trod me in the very dirt
But still like dust, I'll rise . . . .

With the certainty of tides,
Just like hopes springing high,
Still I rise . . ..

.

Does my sexiness upset you?
Does it come as a surprise
That I dance like I've got diamonds
At the meeting of my thighs?

Out of the huts of history's shame
I rise
I rise
I rise.

Finally, I need to express my deepest gratitude to my colleagues and the editors of this book, Jungian analysts Laura Tuley PhD and John White PhD, for their abounding patience with my writing process. I have struggled with efforts to bury this project in layers of ambivalence and procrastination. The topic of the dark feminine and my writing style insisted on finding expression through deeply personal and vulnerable content. To this point, I also want to thank my analysands who have given me their trust and permission to include portions of their own courageous encounters with the dark feminine and their efforts towards healing and individuation.

References

Colonna, M. T. (1980). Lilith, or the black moon. *Journal of Analytical Psychology*, 25(4): 311–337.

Furlotti, N. S. (2017). Encounters with the animal soul: A voice of hope for our precarious world. In T. S. Artzt & M. Asheville (Eds.), *Jung's Red Book for our time: Searching for soul under postmodern conditions*. Chiron Publications.

Gustafson, F. (2003a). The dark mother, the dark earth and the loss of native soul. In F. Gustafson (Ed.), *The moonlit path: Reflections on the dark feminine*. Nicolas-Hays.

Gustafson, F. (2003b). *The moonlit path: Reflections on the dark feminine*. Nicolas-Hays.

Hadas, P. (1976). *The passion of Lilith*. The Cauldron Press.

Irigaray, L. (1997). *This sex which is not one*. Cornell University Press.

Jung, C. G. (1972). Instinct and the unconscious. In R. F. C. Hull (Trans.), *Collected works of C. G. Jung, volume 8*. Princeton University Press.

Kamerling, J. (2003). Lilith. In F. Gustafson (Ed.), *The moonlit path: Reflections on the dark feminine*. Nicolas-Hays.

McNeely, D. A. (1996). *Mercury rising: Women evil and the trickster gods*. Spring Publications.

Meador, B. D. S. (1994). *Uncursing the dark: Treasures from the underworld*. Chiron Publications.

Patai, R. (1990). *The Hebrew goddess* (3rd enl. ed.). Wayne State University Press.

Rowland, S. (2002). *Jung: A feminist revision*. Blackwell.

Stein, M. (2003). Preface. In F. Gustafson (Ed.), *The moonlit path: Reflections on the dark feminine*. Nicolas-Hays.

Van der Kolk, B. A. (2015). *The body keeps the score: Brain mind and body in the healing of trauma*. Penguin Books.

Von Franz, M.-L. (1980). *Alchemy: An introduction to the symbolism and the psychology*. Inner City Books.

Wehr, D. S. (1987). *Jung & feminism: Liberating archetypes*. Beacon Press.

Chapter 4

The View to a Kill

Conscious Cruelty and the Role of Ambivalence in Our Use and Abuse of Non-Human Animals

Laura Camille Tuley

Part I: The Natural Cruelty of the Human Animal

I would like to begin with and ultimately return to myself as a frame for my contemplation on predation and the killing of animals. To circle, you might say, as certain predatory creatures circle their prey. Even before I became conscious of the paradox in my behavior around the consumption of animals, I recognized in myself a sustained fascination with predators and predation. I have, for instance, studied with intense interest and pleasure the nature and rhythms of the great white shark, including its pursuit of its prey. I have reveled in the spectacle of alligator and lion feedings at the zoo, and I have noted the quickening of my pulse in response to a Montana park ranger's tales of grizzly bear maulings. Are these behaviors a kind of "rubber necking," so to speak, in relation to animals eating other animals, or is there something more innate or "instinctive" at play? For it occurs to me that I have also clearly lived as a predator—if largely a "scavenger"—from birth. I have eaten other animals. I have used their bodies for clothing and accessories. I am complicit in their torture through my use of pharmaceuticals and cosmetics. I am, as it were, guilty of the "cruelty" I am poised to pursue. As Marie Von Franz writes, "We shut our eyes to the fact that thousands of animals are butchered so that we may live. To live is to commit murder, and the more intensely I live, the more I commit wrong" (2000, p. 166). The fact and quality of my fascination, however, belie my difference as a human predator from those predators of other species. And this difference bears reflection. It resides in the fact that my sense of exhilaration is often coupled with varying degrees of horror, remorse, and grief. While I recognize the quickening of my pulse at the specter of "the hunt" (the lead-up to and climax in my vicarious experience of death), I also observe my deep and abiding commitment to animal welfare and an awareness of

DOI: 10.4324/9781003252993-5

our vital relation to non-human others. Even before I became conscious of the effective holocaust that constitutes industrialized animal agriculture, I was sensitive to and pained by many of the ways in which domesticated and wild animals are subject to varying degrees of senseless human violence. I would hold the stories left by patients, like offerings at my feet, of pets maimed and killed at the hands of a raging father or alcoholic mother, or sometimes by the patient herself. The trauma survivor, for example, who unveils for me her act of violence as if to say, "Look at, know, and bless my dark heart." I have come to see that when an individual behaves badly, he or she is not, as per the common dictum, behaving like an "animal," but rather behaving like a "human." And therein, I feel, lies the crux of the issue and my own paradoxical relationship to predation. That within the human psyche resides a universal ambivalence that drives us to destroy the world (directly or by proxy) even as it moves us to love and create. It is, if I may speak broadly, out of this fundamental ambivalence that the need for ethics or an ethical stance and related negotiation arises. Non-human animals, on the other hand, are no more "cruel" than they are "ethical." They do not, as far as I can surmise, possess a "shadow" or sadistic capacity, though all animals are capable of violence. The destructiveness of non-human animals is not akin to that of the human's; it does not, for example, resemble that in me which both pleasures in and retreats from predation, because the animal's impulse to kill or maim or even engage in the "torture" of other animals (e.g., the cat) *simply is*. As the novelist Jonathan Safran Foer writes, "[N]ature isn't cruel. And neither are the animals in nature that kill and occasionally even torture one another. Cruelty depends on an understanding of cruelty, and the ability to choose against it" (2009, p. 52). Animal violence is free of ambivalence, without consciousness or conscience.

And so, I continue to circle, as my end is in my beginning.

To repeat: humans are as destructive as we are creative, and violence is neither entirely avoidable nor simply "bad." The generation of life and the movement towards death are, to some degree, always intertwined. Violence can serve life, and death often precedes and engenders birth; those of us familiar with the work of analysis come to know this on a psychological level. To suggest that violent tendencies or destructive potential is only pathological or reflective of an illness or anomaly that can and should be treated or cured is to miss the fundamental complexity that *always* underwrites the human psyche. In his discussion of man's "creative instinct," Jung writes that "creation is as much destruction as construction" (1981,

p. 118), and Sabina Spielrein begins her 1912 article "Destruction as the Cause of Coming into Being" by musing about the seemingly dual nature of the drive to reproduction. "Why," she asks, "does this most powerful drive harbour negative feelings in addition to the inherently anticipated positive feelings?" (1994, p. 155). Spielrein concludes that "Death is horrible; yet death in the service of the sexual instinct [or "life drive"], which includes a destructive component, is a salutary blessing since it leads to a coming into being" (1994, p. 183). The point, as most students and followers of Jung acknowledge, is that the "positive" and the "negative" of psychic and "real" life, or that which spawns and that which kills, not only resist discrete separation but may in fact be interdependent. In "Negative Coniunctio: Envy and Sadomasochism in Analysis," Jungian analyst Pamela Power notes,

> Whether one calls it shadow, trauma, resistance, destructiveness, envy, or narcissism, we recognize that when we invite the forces for psychological growth, integration and individuation to manifest, we also invite the forces of anti-growth, anti-individuation and anti-life. They are inextricably mixed, not just in pathology, but also in life; the only question is what ultimately gets the upper hand.
>
> (2014, p. 1)

Of course, most of us want the energies of growth, individuation, and life to come out on top. But they do not and cannot exist in isolation of their opposites, regardless of the individual or context in question.

Violence can be an end in itself, autonomous and gratifying, not in service of the ego (though it might be in service of something like Jung's "Self")—a force which seeks to create a rift in consciousness and which exists alongside our instinct for life. As the psychoanalyst Jon Mills writes,

> [I]t would be inconceivable to argue that mankind's externalized aggression is not inherently self-destructive for the simple fact that it generates more retaliatory hate, aggression, and mayhem that threatens world accord and the progression of civil societies. Given the global ubiquity of war, genocide and geopolitical atrocities, in all likelihood we as a human race will die by actions brought about by own hands rather than the impersonal forces of nature. *Homo homini lupus*—"Man is a wolf to man."
>
> (2006, p. 373)

This a-teleological human potential for violence is all too often effectively split off and relegated to the unconscious, where it becomes yet more lethal.

Freud's discussion of the topic in his essay "Thoughts for the Times on War and Death," written in 1915, is clear on this count. Here Freud frames the "civilized" human animal's shocking capacity for violence as an expression of our natural yet disavowed "ambivalence of feeling": the fact that "intense love and intense hatred are [so] often to be found together in the same person" (1957, p. 7). The prohibition against murder, he contends, so fundamental to our conception of ourselves as morally different from other animals stems from an innate, if unconscious, recognition of our desire to commit it: "so powerful a prohibition can only be directed against an equally powerful impulse. What no human soul desires stands in no need of prohibition; it is excluded automatically" (1957, p. 19). In other words, we create civilization and corresponding laws and prohibitions in order to delimit our seemingly innate propensity to behave in ways that undermine the survival of human community. That violence still happens nearly everywhere, which the rule of law is ultimately unable to repress or contain, is (or should be) no surprise. One of the conclusions to which Freud returns repeatedly in his essay is the idea that if we were able to create space for and "sublimate" our less savory or personally and socially unacceptable feelings and impulses, they would wreak less havoc for us. An idea that is equally relevant from the perspective of Jung's theory of the "shadow" as that which is opposed to the conscious personality, and which gains energy in the unconscious when denied or repressed, prompting the need for integration.

In his later publication *Civilization and Its Discontents*, Freud again acknowledges the destructive potential and related ambivalence inherent to being human. One's neighbor, for example, is characterized by Freud not only as a potential object of desire or helper but

> also someone who tempts them to satisfy their aggressiveness on him, to exploit his capacity for work without compensation, to use him sexually without his consent, to seize his possessions, to humiliate him, to cause him pain, to torture and to kill him.
>
> (1961, p. 111)

Here it is clear that our acts of cruelty cannot be fully comprehended or circumscribed by theories of defensive structures, trauma, attachment deficits, personality disorder, or mental illness. Rather, the destructive energy embodied in such acts, whether self or other-directed, is, to some extent, *normal*. In the end, Freud boldly cites what many psychologists and psychoanalysts are apt to resist (including, by his own admission, Freud himself): the indisputable evidence of our attraction to violence as an inevitable and incurable fact of the human psyche that creates the need for ongoing negotiation, sublimation, and containment. In *Violence and the Sacred*, literary theorist Rene Girard observes that "violence is not to be denied, but it can be diverted to another object, something it can sink its teeth into" (1977, pp. 3–4). Our aptitude and appetite for bloodshed demand a place at the table of individual and collective life. The questions of how we accord it its place and the nature of that place, however, are crucial, as our expression and uses of violence are most "fitting" or least "cruel" when made conscious.

Part II: "Civilized" Man and his Savage Progression

In *Émile*, his treatise on education and the nature of man, Jean Jacques Rousseau cites man's relation to animals to characterize the difference between "natural man" and "civilized man." He argues that perceived inequalities among men within a "civilized" society are based on the assumption of a natural hierarchy between human and non-human animals. The truth, Rousseau contends, is that social hierarchies, like the hierarchy between man and nature, are based exclusively on the exercise of power (Rousseau, 1979). That is, natural man becomes "civilized" when he assumes power and status over others, a process of identity formation that relies on man's domination of non-human animals as a template:

> [W]e mistreat one another because we mistreat animals. For example, collecting and owning cattle prepares man to collect and own slaves, and from hunting and killing animals man learns war and conquest. Herding cattle teaches men to herd men, hunting wild animals teaches men to hunt men.
>
> (Oliver, 2009, p. 59)

Rousseau's hypothesis was illustrated for me by an exchange with a patient—a self-described "good Catholic" and "family man," who, upon discovering that his dog had "acted out" at doggy day care by biting one of his canine peers, and thereby embarrassing my patient, observed to me, as he contemplated possible remedies, "My dog is my property. If I choose to take it out to the farm and shoot it, that is my prerogative." Not surprisingly, this patient felt a deep sense of shame and loathing towards the "weaker" and unproductive parts of his own personality, which he struggled to marshal to his will.

As a vegetarian, Rousseau believed that "flesh eaters" learned cruelty by virtue of killing and eating other animals, from which their (our) history of domination followed. While Rousseau's conclusions about killing animals and eating meat may sound reductive, our tendency to normalize violence against non-human animals clearly perpetuates a kind of binary opposition (and suggests a foundational splitting) which enables us to mistreat our fellow humans. When humans seek to malign members of their own species, those members are often associated with non-human animals. Consider, for example, the common uses of "chick," "vixen," "cow," "pussy," "shrew," and "bitch" to refer to women, or the frequency with which minority and marginalized groups are targeted as "subhuman" (e.g., slaves, Jews, immigrants, enemies of war, and criminals) (Oliver, 2009). The designation of select humans as "subhuman" or akin to animals of other species not only allows us to rationalize our debasement and abuse of them but reflects our underlying view of the natural supremacy of the human.

In *Living in the Borderland: The Evolution of Consciousness and the Challenge of Healing Trauma*, Jungian analyst Jerome Bernstein contends that the dominion over the earth which western man assumes as his providence has spawned a skewed and reckless relationship to nature, as well as to himself (as part of nature), providing him (us) with a perilous channel through which to exercise his urge to violence. Historically, we human animals do not generally respect or value that which we domesticate, subordinate, and attempt to control, be that the earth, non-human animals, other humans, or the "wilder" dimensions of our own nature. When applied to the arguably pathological treatment of animals within the context of modern agriculture that marks the nexus of our instinct for and the institutionalization of killing animals, Bernstein's analysis of western civilization seems valid, and Rousseau's insight into the character of "civilized man" is darkly prescient.

Traditional Native American thinking about "animal nature" and related cultural practices offers a stark contrast to the legacy of western man's sense of entitlement toward the rest of creation. The Native American scholar

Vine Deloria observes that Sioux stories of their cosmology do not attribute special status to human animals: "All beings are regarded as equals in the presence of the Great Mysterious. In the Sioux belief, man is also created last but not as the ultimate achievement" (Deloria, 2009, p. 115). It was widely held by the Sioux, as well as other Native American communities, that although each kind of animal being possessed its own unique way of adapting to the world, human beings actually shared a great deal in common with other animals, including an innate understanding that, "like humans . . . other creatures had limitations beyond which they could not go" (Deloria, 2009, p. 115). The Sioux saw personality traits in animals and birds that they recognized in themselves. For example, a mother's concern for her young, the expression of bravery in the face of danger, and methods of gathering food or building shelter. Deloria points out that this identification with non-human animal behaviors was not a by-product of anthropomorphizing projections, but rather the result of many years of observation and experience with animals in their native habitats. Moreover, he notes, eventually native peoples realized that other animals possessed knowledge and capacities that humans do not and, for this reason, sought animal "aid" in the tasks and challenges of daily life, a theme one finds in Jung's view of dream animals as "helpers."

Traditional rituals around hunting and fishing further highlight the Native American's sense of connectedness with non-human animals. Through long apprenticeships and experience, native hunters came to know their prey, the topography they traversed, and where and when to hunt within context of the animal's character and habitat. Cajete writes that "techniques of hunting and fishing ranged from simple to complex and required long periods of teaching and learning, but these skills were always learned in the context of a detailed understanding of the natural ecology of tribal homelands" (1994, p. 154). Indigenous hunters also knew and passed on myths, songs, rituals, and history to preserve the attitude and code of behavior associated with the balance and harmony they believed to be essential to their livelihood and health. This painstaking intimacy with and respect for the animals they killed reflected both their community's understanding of its profound dependence on the non-human world and gratitude for what was understood, collectively, as the sacrifice of life in the service of life.

One of the earliest symbols used to represent the indigenous understanding of that sacredness was the "Hunter of Good Heart," an image that suggests a moral code by which human animals are to interact with, approach, and use other beings.

> Among the Pueblo people of the Southwest, the Hunter of Good Heart represented a way of living, a way of relating, a way of ethics and proper behavior, the foundation for teaching and learning about the relationship to animals the Pueblo depended upon for life.
>
> (Cajete, 1994, p. 159)

The teaching process by which the ethics of the Hunter of Good Heart were assimilated began in childhood and extended into old age.

> As the successful Pueblo hunter gathered his extended family to tell the story of the hunt, people listened, and meaning passed from generation to generation as to the way that human beings should conduct themselves with animals, plants and each other.
>
> (Cajete, 1994, p. 159)

Hunting rituals embodied this covenant between the hunter and the hunted.

> In many tribes, there was such identification with animals that not only were hunters' personal names derived from animal experiences or expressions, but entire clans and societies also traced their lineage and their essence of power and social place to animal totems.
>
> (Cajete, 1994, p. 162)

It was believed that the ethics of the Hunter of Good Heart facilitated the development—the "individuation," we might say—of both the hunter and their community as a balanced expression of human animal nature. In other words, paradoxically, the process of becoming fully "human" involved an ongoing recognition of our reciprocal connection to the non-human. And killing other animals was practiced within an ethical and cultural framework that consciously constrained the destructive potential and influence of the human.

This is a strikingly different rapprochement to the world, and to the exercise of violence, than is suggested by the often-unrestrained pursuit of domination that informs us as Judeo-Christian, Western, and "civilized" individuals and communities. It is an ethic that is necessary to adjust and repair the problematic and damaging man/animal (or man/nature) binary that has evolved over millennia, particularly with the evolution of animal husbandry, from the care, cultivation, and breeding of non-human animals to the business of animal agriculture that occupies the shadow of today's "flesh eaters," and which threatens to deplete and destroy all communities of animal life.

Part IV: You Are Who You Eat (And How He or She Lives and Dies)

Much has been written about factory farming, and there is a growing outcry and movement against it. But many Americans remain unconscious of what is happening to the animals that sustain us: how they are raised and killed via methods that can only be described as "torture," how the laborers charged with their "processing" (killing and dismemberment) are also subject to tortuous conditions, how the systematic and large-scale slaughter affects the environment, and the long-term costs to our collective physical and psychological health as consumers of industrial animal "products." This is not entirely our fault; the meat industry works to keep the public in the dark and thereby maintain both its profits and control. According to *The Huffington Post*, despite growing protest, factory farms continue to raise 99.9 percent of meat chickens, 97 percent of laying hens, 99 percent of turkeys, 95 percent of pigs, and 78 percent of cattle currently sold in the United States (Zacharias, 2011, p. 1). Unconscious of and unrelated to the process of how our food (not just animals) is "harvested," we have lost both an important aspect of our "humanity"—our connection to nature—and the ambivalence necessary to mark and check our destruction of that which is not us, but which supports us. It is important that we awaken to the costs of our oblivion and remember the difference between sacrifice and slaughter.

The act of sacrifice, as represented in indigenous hunting practices and related rituals, renders its object "sacred" while exercising and, to an extent, *exorcising* our instinct for violence, whereas slaughter, in its verb form, originally means to "slay wantonly, ruthlessly, or in great numbers" (people or animals). To appreciate this distinction, we need to enlist something more than logic or reason to explain why the large-scale assembly-line killing of animals (or people) is brutally inhumane (while being uniquely "human"), though logic and the use of reason are certainly indispensable here. What is needed, perhaps first, is to awaken a sense of empathy and to cultivate grief, to be taken under by the suffering of others. Not permanently, of course, but for moments (maybe hours or days), to both recognize and experience, ultimately, in order to heal, but also to mourn the loss of the psychological limb we have severed in order to become "civilized": animal being. And to do this we have to look at and listen to the unpalatable reality by which we, in contemporary America, feed ourselves. Jung: "One does not become enlightened by imagining figures of light, but by making the darkness conscious." And to make "the darkness conscious," in Jung's sense, requires an image.

Here are some facts:

On today's factory farms, animals are crammed by the thousands into filthy, windowless sheds and stuffed into wire cages and metal crates. These animals will never raise their young, build nests, root around in the soil, or do anything that is natural or instinctive to them. Most will never feel the warmth of the sun or breathe fresh air until the day they are loaded onto trucks headed for slaughterhouses.

The factory farming industry strives to maximize output while minimizing costs. The multinational corporations that run most factory farms have found that they can make more money by squeezing as many animals as possible into "inhumanely" cramped spaces, even though many of these animals die from disease or infection (PETA).

In the words of Frank Reese, a poultry farmer, "What the industry figured out is that you don't need healthy animals to make a profit. Sick animals are more profitable. The animals have paid the price for our desire to have everything available at all times for very little money" (Foer, 2009, p. 111).

Figure 4.1 Pig behind fence

Figure 4.2 Crated chickens

For example, animals on factory farms endure constant fear and physical torment. Each full-grown chicken in a factory farm has as little as six-tenths of a square foot of space. Because of the crowding, they often become aggressive and sometimes eat each other. This has led to the painful practice of debeaking the birds. Hogs become aggressive in tight spaces and often bite each other's tails, which has caused many farmers to cut the tails off (Organic Consumers Association).

Figure 4.3a Chickens in a factory farm

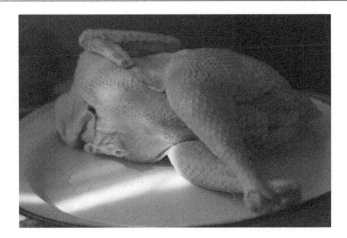

Figure 4.3b Raw chicken on a plate

Sometime between the ages of six months and one year, most beef cattle are sent to live their last few months in crowded feedlots with hundreds or thousands of others. Without pasture and often without shelter, the cattle must stand in mud, ice, and their own waste. Most cows used for dairy production are kept indoors, with some having access to outdoor concrete or dirt paddocks. Many are tethered by chains or other materials around their necks in what are called "tie stalls" (ASPCA).

Figure 4.4 Dairy barn

Antibiotics and growth hormones are used to make animals grow faster and to keep them alive in the unsanitary conditions. This affects the entire food chain adversely. Consuming meat and dairy products containing hormones, antibiotics, pesticides, and dioxins have been found to increase the risk of cancer, heart problems, and other degenerative diseases in humans. Emerging food-borne diseases are causing public and ecosystem health challenges around the world that are often traced back to the industrial animal (Zacharias, 2011, p. 1). Because they have been genetically manipulated to grow larger and to produce more milk or eggs than they naturally would, farm animals often die for reasons related to their body's mutation. Chickens, for example, grow so unnaturally large that their legs cannot support their outsized bodies, and many suffer from starvation or dehydration when they can't walk to reach food and water.

When they've grown large enough to slaughter, or their bodies have been worn out from producing milk or eggs, animals raised for food are crowded onto trucks and transported for miles through all weather extremes, typically without food or water. At the slaughterhouse, those who survived the transport will have their throats slit, often while they're still conscious. Many remain conscious when they're plunged into the scalding-hot water of the defeathering or hair-removal tanks or while their bodies are being skinned or hacked apart. (PETA)

And, as noted previously, it's not just about the suffering of non-human animals. "[I]t is difficult for human beings to subject animals to a gauntlet of violence—no matter how it is rationalized—and not suffer [psychologically]" (McWilliams, 2015, p. 90). Slaughterhouses represent statistically one of the most physically dangerous working environments in the country.

When the main tool of your trade is a knife honed to cut bone like butter, and when the pace of work requires you to make accurate cuts every three seconds for eight hours a day, chances are good—in fact they're 51%—that you'll end up hurt. It's no wonder that slaughterhouse turnover rates are commonly 200% for first-time workers. The psychological scars can be equally painful.

One study concludes, "Slaughterhouse work is very likely to have a serious, negative psychological impact on the employees." Given that mental health professionals (and most of the general public) view animal torture as a symptom of psychosis, it stands to reason that workers who witness systematic violence against helpless animals—minute after minute, day after day—develop mental illness. They may react in a myriad of ways: by brutalizing animals at work, drinking excessively at home, becoming emotionally disengaged, or engaging in antisocial behaviors that impact the surrounding community.

(McWilliams, 2015, pp. 91–92)

The influence of a slaughterhouse on local communities is invariably negative. "'Slaughterhouse employment increases total arrest rates, arrest rates for violent crimes, arrests for rape, and arrests for other sex offenses in comparison with other industries'" (McWilliams, 2015, p. 92). The reason for this is clearly the damaging effect of this work and environment on the human psyche.

Figure 4.5 Slaughterhouse worker on break

As one worker recounts:

> The worst thing, worse than the physical danger, is the emotional toll. If you work in the stick pit for any period of time, you develop an attitude that lets you kill things but doesn't let you care. You may look a hog in the eye that's walking around down in the blood pit with you and think, God, that really isn't a bad-looking animal. You may want to pet it. Pigs down on the kill floor have come up and nuzzled me like a puppy. Two minutes later I had to kill them—beat them to death with a pipe. . . . When I worked upstairs taking hogs' guts out, I could cop an attitude that I was working on a production line, helping to feed people. But down in the stick pit I wasn't feeding people. I was killing things.

(Foer, 2009, p. 254)

And then there's the damage to the environment. According to many sources, animal agriculture makes a 40% greater contribution to global warming than all transportation in the world combined; it is the number one

Figure 4.6 Factory farm

cause of climate change (Foer, 2009, p. 43). In and of itself, the waste that is produced by the industry represents an ecological crisis:

> All told, farmed animals in the United States produce 130 times as much waste as the human population—roughly 87,000 pounds of shit per second. The polluting strength of this shit is 160 times greater than raw municipal sewage. And yet there is almost no waste treatment infrastructure for farmed animals—no toilets, obviously, but also no sewage pipes, no one hauling it away for treatment, and almost no federal guidelines regulating what happens to it.
>
> (Foer, 2009, p. 174)

So what happens to all of that waste? It is pumped into lagoons that often leak into waterways, and poisonous gases like ammonia and hydrogen sulfide evaporate into the air. When the football-field-sized cesspools are approaching overflowing, companies like Smithfield, for example, spray the liquefied manure onto fields. Or sometimes they simply spray it straight up into the air, a geyser of shit wafting fine fecal mists that create swirling gases capable of causing severe neurological damage. Communities living near these factory farms complain about problems with persistent nosebleeds, earaches, chronic diarrhea, and burning lungs. Even when citizens have passed laws that would restrict these practices, the industry's immense influence in government means the regulations are often nullified or go unenforced (Foer, 2009, pp. 177–178).

I could go on. All of this is just the tip of the iceberg. Nil Zacharias of One Green Planet wrote in *The Huffington Post*,

> This is not just an animal welfare or environmental concern, it's also a humanitarian crisis, because factory farms are diverting precious natural resources like land, water and fossil fuels to raise farm animals, while millions of people around the world are malnourished and still do not have access to safe drinking water.
>
> (2011, p. 1)

Our appetite for plentiful cheap meat and our psychological and physical detachment from animal agriculture has enabled a profoundly cruel and destructive industry to flourish. And it seems that the American desire and associated demand for meat has accelerated with the advent of the assembly line. According to Foer, "On average, Americans eat the equivalent of 21,000 entire animals in a lifetime" (2009, p. 121). In an interview with *The Washington Post* in 2009, Foer noted,

> We now raise 50 billion animals in factory farms every year. If China and India take up our eating habits—and the world population doesn't increase at all—we will have to raise twice as many animals. There simply isn't enough land on earth to humanely and sustainably farm the amount of meat we 'want' to eat. Americans now eat 150 times as much chicken as we did 80 years ago. Hard to call that radical a change a "consumer preference."

If, as I would claim, our treatment of non-human animals is a barometer of our management of the "death instinct" we all harbor within us, I have to conclude that we, as a collective, are managing it poorly.

In his prescient novel, *The Jungle*, Upton Sinclair observed the dehumanizing effects of the assembly line that enabled an unconscious meat-eating public to remain happily oblivious to the horror that produced its food. This was at the turn of the twentieth century, well before animal processing factories were relocated from densely packed urban centers to remote rural communities, out of the sight and smell of most Americans. Before the development of CAFO's (Concentrated Animal Feeding Operations). Before McDonald's. What, in fact, initially inspired him to write about the urban packing yard was a concern for alienated labor and an affinity for Karl Marx, not the quality of the meat or the suffering of animals. In so doing, however, it was impossible not to refer to the treatment of the animal, and Sinclair used that treatment, if in part metaphorically, to make his case. In his novel, Sinclair makes what are at times sentimentalized but nevertheless pointed efforts to call the reader's attention to the exploitation and effective killing of the meatpacker through analogy with the suffering of the animal on the industrial assembly line. Human animals are often moved by other animals when they appear to be *more like us* (i.e., more human). Sinclair takes aim at this proclivity in his novel to pull on the reader's "heartstrings" and, as I have suggested, to develop an analogy between the system's treatment of one sentient being (the pig) and another (the blue-collar worker). But in so doing, he cannot help but call attention to a brutalizing, if at this point fledgling, method of killing animals. In this way, Sinclair connects us not just with the evils of capitalism (which he does effectively) but with the "evil" in ourselves, as consumers who devour our fellow human and animal beings "relentlessly" and "remorselessly," and who prefer *not* dwell on where our food comes from at great cost to others and ourselves, as he challenges a meat industry that is happy to oblige us in our unconscious cruelty by systematically disguising the relationship of the animal to the meat on our plate.

Beginning in Cincinnati and expanding to Chicago by the late 1820s and '30s, early industrial processing plants (i.e., slaughterhouses) supplanted skilled butchers with crews of men who would perform a coordinated series of uniform tasks. "Kill men, sticker bleeders, tail-rippers, leggers, butters, flankers, head-skinners, head-chiselers, gutters and back splitters (among many others)" (Foer, 2009, p. 103). The efficiency of these lines inspired Henry Ford, who imported the model to the auto industry, where it earned him widespread success. The pressure to increase efficiency coincided with advances in rail transport, and the invention of the refrigerator car in 1879, which enabled large concentrations of cattle to be transported from ever-increasing distances. Today, it is common for meat to travel to your local supermarket from almost halfway around the globe. The conveyer belt was introduced to the process of animal production by 1908, allowing supervisors (rather than workers) to control the speed of production. Foer notes that "[t]hese speeds would ramp upward for more than eighty years—in many cases doubling and even tripling—with predictable increases in ineffective slaughter and associated work-place injuries" (Foer, 2009, p. 104).

The literary critic Maura Spiegel cites the historian Siegfried Giedion who argues in *Mechanization Takes Command* that the assembly line system "imparts a distinct neutrality to the act of killing" (Giedion, 1969, xiv), but adds that unlike the production of inanimate objects, the slaughter of animals can never be completely mechanized. "Only the knife, guided by the human hand, can perform the transition from life to death in the desired manner" (Sinclair, 2003, p. xx). What *is* increasingly neutralized, however, is the consumer's link to the act of killing and the suffering of his or her victim. Only the "happy meal" remains to bolster our denial. We don't think about their suffering because we don't have to. Thus, an elaborate system of torture and our participation in it remains both invisible and unchecked.

Figure 4.7 Fast-food burger

To summarize, what was enabled intellectually and psychologically by a sense of dominion and reinforced by our legal and physical ownership of other animals ("animal husbandry") has, with the aid of post-industrialized capitalism, devolved into unmitigated barbarity. Farming was not, in its original form, a gentle profession (the goal, after all, was the same). But it was not without compassion, albeit paternalistic. In *The Omnivore's Dilemma*, Michael Pollan reflects a common line of thinking about domestication which suggests that it is the natural product of a coevolution between human animals and animals of other species. Basically, the thinking goes: you provide us with your resources, animals, and, in exchange, we, humans, will take care of you. That is, until we kill you. Implicit in this view is something like the animal's consent. Pollan puts a positive and somewhat romanticized spin on an arrangement that, in the last century, has, without question, generated more pain, illness, and suffering for domesticated animals than it has an experience of "care" (and Pollan, who has championed the fight against factory farming, would not disagree with this; he would simply attribute the problem to more recent formations, rather than something inherent in the arrangement itself). Foer, on the other hand, concludes that

> we have let the factory farm replace farming for the same reason our cultures have relegated minorities to being second-class members of Society

and kept women under the power of men. We treat animals as we do because we want to and can. The myth of consent is perhaps *the* story of meat, and much comes down to whether this story, when we are realistic, is plausible.

(Foer, 2009, p. 243)

What farm animals endure today is neither a good deal nor the kind of sacrifice implied by traditional hunting rituals. It is a holocaust.

We need to make space, psychologically, for the specter of our relationship to other animals, in all of its dirt, if we are to curb their wholesale slaughter and slow our fast-track assembly line to *self*-annihilation. As Freud asks in 1915, "Would it not be better to give death the place in reality and in our thoughts which is its due?" Would it not be better, in other words, to associate with the "predator" within—to name, know, and limit our impulse towards violence—than to allow it to gain psychopathic proportion in the unconscious feedlots of our individual and collective psyches? Lily Raff McCaulou, a journalist and hunter, writes in her memoir *Call of the Mild*, very much in the spirit of the indigenous hunter of good heart,

I promise myself that if I ever get to the point where I kill an animal and don't feel in awe of it . . . don't feel twinges of guilt upon reflection or . . . don't feel grateful for its life, then I will stop.

(2012, p. 296)

Figure 4.8 Pig in crate

It is this critical sense of conscious ambivalence—missing for most of us in our acquisition and consumption of animals—that I strive to recall.

Conclusion: The Analytic Practice of Tikkun Olam

I began this writing with a profound conviction, one that emerged within the context of my life, clinical practice, and training in post-Katrina New Orleans, that human animals are uniquely violent and naturally cruel, as destructive as they are creative, sometimes in the service of a particular telos or growth, but often simply because we human creatures, by our very nature, break things and others, often without rational cause or discernable goal, *because we can*. But also that we can awaken consciousness and with it our capacity to choose ethically—which could, in this case, include a range of options such as eating less animal protein or buying animal protein from local and small family farms, choosing meat alternatives, protesting factory farms on the policy or regulatory level, and perhaps, for some, hunting one's food with an ethical awareness of the animal's role in the ecosystem that some hunters possess. None of these choices will interrupt the damaging role of capitalism, "fix" the system, or, for that matter, dampen the human urge to kill. But they might alter the individual's relationship to their environment and, by extension, to themselves, a change that could in turn affect an evolution in the collective's consciousness.

One might ask, why is my focus on the killing of non-human animals, when so many human animals suffer from violence and abuse? Are human animals not, in other words, a more urgent priority, particularly as our analytic work is focused on people? I feel that I have answered this question in proposing that our relation to killing and using animals represents a kind of snapshot of our general mental health. But I would also note that this is the wrong question, a question that reflects the logic of dominion. If we were to view ourselves and the world we inhabit as interconnected, we would not consider the ethical treatment of other human animals and non-human animals or the environment as mutually exclusive but, rather, as fundamentally intertwined. I have frequently heard stories in my consulting room of cruelty and violence towards non-human animals (typically pets), which, in my experience, often accompany stories of human abuse (typically of children). Were we to integrate a notion of "animal rights" alongside the priority of "human rights," or, moreover, to consider "animal rights" to include the human as well as the non-human, I suspect, one would hear many more tales of cruelty to non-human animals in one's consulting room, and the underlying need to tend to their wounding, just as we are hearing, if we listen, the grief and anxiety that growing evidence of climate change exacts from the psyche.

Bernstein highlights the value of mourning our destruction of the earth through his exchange with a patient who suffered for the pain of animals, the loss of nature, and the "choking-off of instinct." "It matters," Bernstein tells him, "because your mourning appreciates the people and places you love, the wolf, the elk, the choking earth—and thanks them for their being" (Bernstein, 2005, p. 77). One does not need to look far for the wisdom of grief. Our personal and collective sadness is, in and of itself, vital and healing; like the ambivalence that connects us at once to our capacities for cruelty and compassion, our mourning reconnects us with the world we have plundered, often unwittingly, in our desire for life. But re-association with the fullness of our nature is painful, and there is much inducement in contemporary culture to numb or sedate rather than suffer the pain of consciousness. Bernstein writes,

> I have come to the conclusion over the past fifteen years that the collective unconscious has tapped certain individuals within the culture to be carriers of personal and collective mourning for the profound assault and wounds to nature wrought, predominantly, by western civilization and the modern technological society.
>
> (2005, p. 79)

The idea that certain individuals might be "tapped" by the collective unconscious to carry and grieve the wounds of the earth and its inhabitants is reassuring to me, regardless of whether this expression of grief is able to reverse or redeem the violence of history. It is not unlike the vocation of the analyst who carries, even as she interprets, the wounding of her patient. And yet, this is a responsibility that we cannot afford to relegate to the few, as it is as basic and common as the choices we make at the breakfast and dinner table each day, choices in which all of us share. I suggest that we meet the darkness in ourselves and our world as we might meet those carriers of despair when they show up in our consulting rooms and call us to surrender—momentarily—to the deep ambivalence of human being.

Sonnets to Orpheus II, 29

Quiet friend who has come so far,
feel how your breathing makes more space around you.
Let this darkness be a bell tower
and you the bell. As you ring,

what batters you becomes your strength.
Move back and forth into the change.
What is it like, such intensity of pain?
If the drink is bitter, turn yourself to wine.

In this uncontainable night,
be the mystery at the crossroads of your senses,
the meaning discovered there.

And if the world has ceased to hear you,
say to the silent Earth: I flow.
To the rushing water, speak: I am.
　　　　　—Rainer Maria Rilke, translation by Joanna Macy
　　　　　　　　　　　　　　and Anita Barrows

References

Bernstein, Jerome S. (2005). *Living in the Borderland: The Evolution of Consciousness and the Challenge of Healing Trauma*. Routledge.

Cajete, Gregory. (1994). *Look to the Mountain: An Ecology of Indigenous Education*. Kivaki Press.

Deloria, Vine, Jr. (2009). *C.G. Jung and the Sioux Traditions: Dreams, Visions, Nature, and the Primitive*. Spring Journal Books.

Foer, Jonathan Safran. (2009). *Eating Animals*. Bay Back Books/Little, Brown and Company.

Freud, Sigmund. (1961). *Civilization and Its Discontents*. Translated by James Strachey. Norton.

———. (1957). *Thoughts for the Times on War and Death*. Translated by James Strachey, in Collaboration with Anna Freud. The Hogarth Press and the Institute of Psycho-Analysis.

Giedion, Siegfried. (1969). *Mechanization Takes Command*. W.W. Norton & Company.

Girard, René. (1977). *Violence and the Sacred*. Translated by Patrick Gregory. The Johns Hopkins University Press.

Jung, C. G. (1981). *The Structure and Dynamics of the Psyche*. Translated by R. F. C. Hull. The Collected Works of C. G. Jung, Volume 8: Bollingen Series XX. Princeton University Press.

McCaulou, Lily Raff. (2012). *Call of the Mild: Learning to Hunt My Own Dinner*. Grand Central Publishing.

McWilliams, James. (2015). *The Modern Savage*. St Martin's Press.

Mills, Jon. (2006). Reflections on the death drive. *Psychoanalytic Psychology*, 3: 373–382.

Oliver, Kelly. (2009). *Animal Lessons: How They Teach Us to Be Human*. Columbia University Press.

Power, Pamela. (2014). Negative coniunctio: Envy and sadomasochism in analysis. In *Participation Mystique*. Edited by Mark Winborn. Fisher King Press.

Rousseau, Jean-Jacques. (1979). *Émile: Or on Education*. Translated by Allan Bloom. Basic Books.

Sinclair, Upton. (2003). *The Jungle*. Barnes & Noble Classics.

Spielrein, Sabina. (1994). Destruction as the cause of coming into being. *Journal of Analytical Psychology*, 39: 155–186.

Von Fran, Marie-Louise. (2000). *The Problem of the Puer Aeternus*. Inner City Books.

Zacharias, Nil. (2011). It's time to end factory farming. *The Huffington Post.*

Chapter 5

Cuauhtémoc and the Other

Confronting the Chingada Complex

Jorge de la O

My family and I were living in Spain during the 500th-anniversary celebration of Christopher Columbus' arrival in North America. We were at the World's Fair in Sevilla, visiting an exhibition of the caves of Lascaux, France. Imagine for a moment a large room converted into a replica of those prehistoric caves. It was done in such a way that one could feel the sacredness of the caves and the prehistoric wall paintings. As I listened to the commentary, the background voice turned its attention to Rome, the "discovery of America," and the Vatican of 1537. The audio informed us that the debate of the time was, "Did the Indians of America have souls?" Something stirred in me and brought great sorrow. It was later that I discovered Uruguayan journalist Eduardo Galeano's trilogy, *Memory of Fire*, which informs us that Pope Paul III had issued a papal bull stating that the Indians of the Americas were human beings just like the Europeans. The papal bull also states that the indigenous of the Americas had a soul and a mind.

In sixteenth-century Europe, it was widely held that the soul only belonged to those who were part of the Christian Church through baptism and the other holy sacraments. In 1547, Juan Ginés de Sepúlveda, Spanish philosopher, and theologian, argued before the Spanish court that Native Americans were "the barbarians of the New World, and nothing healthier could have occurred to these barbarians than to be subject to the empire" (Fuentes, 1992). In contrast, Dominican friar Bartolomé de las Casas argued for the humanity of the indigenous people. He accused the conquistadors of "endless crimes and offenses against the Indians who were the king's subject" (Fuentes, 1992). While it is true that many friars in the Americas treated the indigenous population with compassion and goodwill, the fact remains that the indigenous people were not saved from the oppression and brutality of the Spanish conquest. The indigenous populations in the

DOI: 10.4324/9781003252993-6

Americas were ultimately treated as inferior subjects to be bought, sold, and subjugated. It must be noted that the indigenous population was decimated. It is estimated that the population in Central Mexico in 1520 was at 25 million; by the beginning of the seventeenth century, the indigenous population was approximately 1.3 million. In less than a century, 24 million people died from disease, slavery, or murder. As I listened to the narrative of that summer's day in Sevilla, I was moved to tears, and a wave of deep-seated anger took possession of me.

Europe would collide with the imaginal world of the Indigenous Americas. The European discovery of the Americas would challenge Europe's understanding of the planet's geography and what it meant to be considered as human. That debate unconsciously, and not so unconsciously, continues today in the form of social injustice, racism, and immigration policies.

James Hillman argued that Europe's connection to classical Greece and the Renaissance was becoming implausible and the European Enlightenment was transforming the world into one based on reason and literalism. Hillman writes,

> Renaissance animism led to pluralism, which threatened Christian universal harmony. For when inner soul and outer world reflect each other as enlivened souls and substances, and when the images of these souls and substances are pagan, then the familiar figures of Christianity diminish to only one relative set among many alternatives.
>
> (Hillman, 1977, p. 4)

It was an epoch when the imaginal view of life would be damned as demonism; this attitude would find itself on the caravels that sailed west to the Americas. Hillman (1977) goes on to write,

> Soul was confined to the persons of Christ and those baptized in his name, all else burnt out of Being or moving mechanically around a clockwork orbit. Animals were bereft of psyche, and children, even when baptized, did not have the full reality of souls. Both modern science as it was then being formed and modern Christianity as it was then being reformed, required that subjectivities be purged from everywhere and everything except the authorized place of persons: the rational Christian adult.
>
> (p. 5)

Christian-Cartesian Alliance

In addition to the handiwork of the church, Descartes' view of the world altered beliefs about humanity's relationship to objects in the universe and nature itself. Professor and author Richard Tarnas explains,

> The Newton-Cartesian cosmology was now established as the foundation for a new world view. By the beginning of the 18th century the educated person in the west knew that God had created the universe as a complex mechanical system, composed of material particles moving in an infinite neutral space according to a few basic principles, such as inertia and gravity, that could be analyzed mathematically . . . man's role in that universe could best be judged on the evidence that, by ritual of his own intelligence, he had penetrated the universe's essential order and could now use that knowledge for his own benefit and empowerment. One could scarcely doubt that man was the crown of creation the scientific revolution and the birth of the modern era—was now complete.
> (Tarnas, 2011, p. 270)

We find a belief system that has no room for anything in between. The Cartesian view of life danced hand in hand with the early modern Christian attack on the imaginal world. In the final analysis, the Christian-Cartesian alliance led to the end of a conscious symbolic view of the universe in Europe. This Cartesian-Christian view would lead to the destruction of the great civilizations in the so-called "New World." It meant destruction for Amerindian ways of knowing and the sacred connection to plants, animals, and the universe.

The Chingada Complex

Jung's trip to New Mexico and subsequent meeting with Hopi Elder Ochwiay Biano in 1925 led to his realization of the many generations of suffering and oppression:

> For the first time in my life, so it seemed to me, someone had drawn for me a picture of the real white man. It was as though until now I had seen nothing but sentimental, prettified color prints. This Indian had struck our vulnerable spot, unveiled a truth to which we are blind. I felt rising within me like a shapeless mist something unknown and yet deeply

familiar. And out of this mist, image upon image detached itself: first Roman legions smashing into the cities of Gaul, and the keenly incised features of Julius Caesar, Scipio Africanus, and Pompey. I saw the Roman Eagle on the North Sea and on the banks of the White Nile.

Then I saw St. Augustine transmitting the Christian creed to the Britons on the tips of Roman lances, and Charlemagne's most glorious, forced conversions of the heathen, then the pillaging and murdering bands of the Crusading armies. With a secret stab I realized the hollowness of that old romanticism about the Crusades. Then followed Columbus, Cortés, and the other conquistadors who with fire, sword, torture and Christianity came down upon even these remote pueblo.

It was enough. What we from our point of view call colonization, missions to the heathen, the spread of civilization, etc. has another face—the face of a bird of prey seeking with cruel intentness for distant quarry—a face worthy of a race of pirates and highwaymen. All the eagles and other predatory creatures that adorn our coats of arms seem to me apt psychological representatives of our true nature.

(Jung, 2011, p. 248)

In this excerpt from *Memories, Dreams and Reflections*, Jung speaks to a cultural complex found in the Americas. The Conquest of Mexico has been referred to as *"La Gran Chingada."* The verb *"Chingar"* is very much a part of the Mexican lexicon. A working definition for *Chingada* is "to be violated." *La Chingada* is about tyranny, and it is about exploitation, violence, and slavery which is rooted in the Conquest of Mexico. A portrait of this catastrophe and its mythical significance is revealed in the martyrdom of the last *tlatoani* (emperor) of the Mexica. *La Chingada* is about irrevocable loss. This cultural complex, the Chingada Complex, is a direct result of the Conquest, which began in 1492. (de La O, 2020)

El Fantasma

Images of the Conquest of the Americas came to me that day in Sevilla. I could not help but remember the atrocities of the Conquest in the name of Christ and imperious greed. I recalled the stories my mother would tell me about the "Aztecs." She also would say to me that my great uncle claimed Aztec ancestry. Since childhood, I have had many dreams of ancient Mexico and of what I assumed was Tenochtitlán, an ethereal image that has been with me since childhood. I must add that I feel very removed from Mexico and my ancestorial roots, yet my dreams have been obsessed with indigenous images.

Samuel Kimbles informs us that cultural complexes are intergenerational and, over time, become phantoms. They are present, as is evident from my experience in Sevilla. Kimbles writes:

> At the level of the unconscious, certain kinds of images (phantoms) and affects that appear in the aftermath of natural and social catastrophes are representations of unconscious narratives (phantom narratives) expressing the inner psychological dimensions of culture's working interiority. These phantoms come with an underlying narrative structure . . . which show how the unconscious, working at the group and individual levels, provides intergenerational, political, and social contexts within which both individuals and groups may find a different kind of emotional containment for these catastrophes. In this way suffering may be potentially processed psychologically and related to symbolically.
>
> (Kimbles, 2021, p. 1)

El Encuentro

The story of the Conquest of Mexico remains an unprocessed psychological trauma that is active in the Mexican and collective Latinx psyche. The indigenous world of the Mexica (Aztecs) of Central Mexico was mythological. Mexican author and essayist Carlos Fuentes wrote that "myth was the interpretation that explained reality" for the Mexica (Fuentes, 1992, p. 94). Mythos was inseparable from day-to-day life for the Mexica of Mexico. Their deities caused everything good and bad in life. The Gods had lived with the Indigenous of Central Mexico for six thousand years before Christ. The polytheistic world of the Mexica at the time of the Conquest was all-encompassing.

In contrast, under the Catholic monarchs Fernando II de Aragón and Isabel de Castilla, Spain would expel the Jews and defeat the Moors in Granada, thus unifying the country under one God and one religion in 1492. As Fuentes saw it, "it became the central question of the Americas, as Spain encountered the radically Other—people of another race, another religion, another culture." Who were these people? What was the shape of their souls? Did they even have souls?" (Fuentes, 1992, p. 88).

Confronting the Other

The question of the "Other" now confronts analytical psychology with renewed urgency. The Jungian tradition is at a crossroads and must see the "Other" with renewed vision. This new lens must include the cultural level of the psyche found in the Americas. Western depth psychology is at an intersection that demands a reimagining of the unconscious that honors the cultural unconscious of People of Color.

This cultural unconscious includes not only the collective legacy of the Conquest but is infused with a history of colonialism and violence that impacts People of Color today. Jungian analyst John Hill (as cited in Gudait and Stein, 2014) reminds us that "the history of our civilization has unfortunately been a storehouse of innumerable examples of cultural trauma."

Thomas Singer, in *The Cultural Complex*, suggests that cultural trauma leads to cultural complexes:

> Intense collective emotion is the hallmark of an activated cultural complex at the core of which is an archetypal pattern. Cultural complexes structure emotional experience and operate in the personal and collective psyche in much the same way as individual complexes, although their content might be quite different. Like individual complexes, cultural complexes tend to be repetitive, autonomous, resist consciousness, and collect experience that confirms their historical point of view.
>
> (Singer, 2004, p. 6)

A Latin-American Duality

However, the culture of Spain is multicultural; the Spaniards are of mixed ethnic and racial birth. At the time of the Conquest, Spain was driven by a desire for power and the establishment of Christianity as the country's sole religion. This multicultural lineage was in place with the arrival of Spain to the Americas. Nobel Prize–winning poet Octavio Paz tells us that Spain was "still a medieval nation" (Paz, p. 97). In other words, the conquistadors were themselves a mixture of cultural and religious backgrounds. Carlos Fuentes (1992) writes that this dilemma would also sail with Hernán Cortés.

> Ferdinand and Isabella were driven by a single-minded vision of Christian unity, reconquest, and expansion. Undoubtedly, their captains and

soldiers overseas share this vision. But they were also the heirs to a multicultural experience of coexistence, of comingling in tension with the Jews and with the Moors. All the exceptions to the tolerance cannot detract the fact that the tendencies towards coexistence with and respect for others did structure a tricultural reality, which stood in stark contrast to the official policy of expulsion and denial of Jews and moors.

The conquerors of the New World were a part of this reality, they could not squirm away from the choice of Spain. Their friars, writers, chroniclers, and polemicists who followed the conquistadors saw to it that Spain faced its humanistic and multicultural alternative.

(p. 89)

It can also be argued that Spain's multicultural heritage has preserved the very existence of the Indigenous culture in Latin America. Once again, turning to Carlos Fuentes reminds us that if we are to know ourselves (the Mexican), we must know Spain:

It was through Spain that the Americas first received the full sweep of the Mediterranean tradition, for Spain is not only Christian but Arab and Jewish, she is also great, Carthaginian, Roman, and both Gothic and Gypsy. We might have a more powerful Indian tradition in Mexico, Guatemala, Ecuador, Peru, and Bolivia; or a stronger European presence in Argentina, or Chile; or a stronger black tradition in the Caribbean, Venezuela, and Columbia then in Mexico or Paraguay. But Spain embraces all of us; he is in a way, our commonplace, our common ground. *La Madre Patria*, the Mother Fatherland.

(p. 15)

Latinx communities continue to have an active psychological connection between their Iberian legacy and the American Indigenous. The connection to the ancestral psyche is not lost but continues to haunt (and nourish) the people of the Americas consciously and unconsciously.

Jung would write about the Cartesian-Christian attitude which brought destruction and imbalance to the Americas and to the world in the following way, "We are awakening a little to the feeling that something is wrong in the world, that our modern prejudice of overestimating the importance of the intellect and the conscious mind might be false" (Jung, 1978, p. 49).

La Chingada includes the factual events that occurred during the Age of Exploration, but moves into the realm of the mythical to reveal the darkness of the human soul. *"La Gran Chingada,"* has possessed the soul of the Americas. Jungians and others in depth psychology must not only concern themselves with the wounding of individuals but with the wounding of the Latinx psyche and thus come to terms with the Chingada on the collective trauma of Brown people. The events of 1521 are not long-forgotten events but reveal the anguish and sorrow of a collective trauma rooted in colonialism. Kimbles writes that by paying "attention to group complexes, we may come into a better relationship with the autonomy of the psyche as it plays itself out at individual and cultural levels, expressed as collective myths, images, and themes" (Kimble, 2021, p. 8).

It has become imperative that depth psychology take the history of the Americas and its associated traumatic wounding seriously and revitalize Jung's belief that the "psyche does not merely react; it gives its own specific answer to the influences at work upon it" (Jung, 1961, p. 287). The question is what are these "specific answers," and what are the influences at work? I suggest that "what is wrong in the world" is held in the horrendous history of colonialism. Once again, it is imperative that depth psychology consciously acknowledge the impact of colonialism on the psyche of the Americas.

Cuauhtémoc

The final conquest of Mexico occurred in 1521, and the last *tlatoani* of the Mexica, Cuauhtémoc, lives in the hearts of the Mexican and Chicanx souls. We will examine the figure of Cuauhtémoc as an example of how the trauma of the Conquest continues to be present in the collective psyche of Mexico.

In 1520, Hernán Cortés and his men had taken control of Tenochtitlán. Moctezuma, the emperor of the Mexica, had been taken prisoner by Cortés. As the Spanish tell it, he was stoned to death by his people for collaboration with the conquistadors. After Moctezuma's death, Cortés made Cuauhtémoc emperor of the Mexica. Soon after, Hernán Cortés would order Cuauhtémoc tortured in the hopes that the young monarch would reveal the rumored hidden treasures of the Mexica. The torture of Cuauhtémoc has become a living psychic symbol (Figure 5.1).

Figure 5.1 Leonadro Izaquirre, **1892**

Cuauhtémoc is both heroic and tragic. He was tortured along with others. While he was being tortured, Cuauhtémoc is reputed to have said, "Am I myself in a pleasant bath?" (Fehrenbach, 1995). His suffering and his bold defiance have become symbolic of our suffering due to exploitation and oppression of human rights. Cortés' action must also be understood as the maiming and disfiguring of the indigenous peoples' connection to the Earth and perhaps has defaced it forever.

Cuauhtémoc led his people in revolt against the *conquistadores*, known today as "*La Noche Triste*," and temporarily recaptured the city. Cuauhtémoc would be taken prisoner by the Spaniards in the final battle for Tenochtitlán (Mexico City) in 1521, two years after his uncle Montezuma had welcomed the Spaniards to the capital.

The world is silenced in the rain

Galeano writes:

Suddenly, all at once, the cries of the drums cease. Gods and men have been defeated. With the gods' death, time has died. With the men's death, the city has died. This warrior city, she of white willows and white rushes, has died fighting as she lived. No more will conquered princes of all regions come in boats through the mist to pay her tribute.

A stunning silence reigns. And the rain begins to fall. Thunder and lightning fill the sky, and it rains all through the night. Gold is piled into huge baskets. Gold shields and insignia of war, gold of the masks of gods, lips and ear pendants, ornaments, lockets. The gold is weighed and the prisoners priced. *One of these wretches is hardly worth two handfuls of corn. . . .* The soldiers gathered to play dice and cards.

Fires burn the soles of the Emperor Cuauhtémoc's feet anointed with oil, while the world is silent, and it rains.

> (Galeano and Belfrage, 1985, pp. 71–72)

In a final degradation, Cortés orders Cuauhtémoc hung because of an alleged plot against the Spaniards. Cuauhtémoc was suspended by the feet and decapitated from a Ceiba tree. It is an image that continues to torment the hearts and minds of the Mexican and the Chicanx. It is also a figure of deep and passionate pride. Octavio Paz, in *Labyrinth of Solitude*, tells us of the mythical power of this story:

He (Cuauhtémoc) is a warrior, but he is also a child. The exception is that the heroic cycle does not end with the death: the fallen hero awaits resurrection. It is not surprising that for the majority of Mexicans, Cuauhtémoc should be "the young grandfather," the origin of Mexico: the hero's tomb is the cradle of the people. This is the dialectic of the myth, and Cuauhtémoc is more a myth than a historical figure.

> (Paz, 1962, p. 84)

In defeat, the last *tlatoani* would become a national hero (Figure 5.2). His story is mythical. Beyond the account surrounding his downfall, the story of Cuauhtémoc intersects with the collective archetype of the fallen warrior. Cuauhtémoc, whose name translates as "Descending Eagle," is the sacred martyr. Jung says the act of naming is,

like baptism, extremely important as regards the creation of personality, for a magical power has been attributed to the name since time immortal. Therefore, to give a name means to give power, to invest with a definite personality or soul.

> (Jung, 1969, p. 187)

How might we understand Cuauhtémoc's naming? Perchance his naming at birth was prophetic, a foretelling of future events. His name is also

Figure 5.2 Photo taken by Estela Bobadilla, 2022

understood to mean "one who descends like an eagle," thus implying a graceful but powerful descent, a *coniunctio* between the heavens to the earthly world of man. By amplifying the mythos of Cuauhtémoc, we can begin to understand the transgenerational cultural complex found in the Americas. Kimbles (2021) highlights this dynamic in the following passage:

> Transgenerational complexes bring past and present together within a current sociopolitical context. The cultural past brings with it ghosts that represent the unacknowledged harm done through violence to the selves of the exploited, denigrated, and colonized other.

(p. 4)

The Ceiba Tree

As stated earlier, Cuauhtémoc was hung from a ceiba tree, which is, for the Mexica and the Maya, the sacred world tree. Professor and archaeologist Nicoletta Maestri informs us that

> the ceiba was the most sacred tree for the ancient Maya, and according to Maya mythology, it was the symbol of the universe. The tree signified a route of communication between the three levels of earth. Its roots were said to reach down into the underworld, its trunk represented the middle world where the humans live, and its canopy of branches arched high in the sky symbolized the upper world and the thirteen levels in which the Maya heaven was divided.
>
> (Maestri, 2019)

A parallel can be made with the crucifixion of Christ. Like the Christian cross, the tree symbolizes the union of the opposites, where the roots reach down, and the branches seek the heavens above. Both images symbolize life, death, and rebirth. Then again, there is nothing aesthetic in the hanging of a Person of Color or the crucifixion of Christ. As I write this, I am reminded of the history of lynching in the United States. I am in fear that I am slipping once again back to romantic European mythology. We must not forget the brutal side of the human psyche that has manifested in the form of racism. In my mind, I can hear jazz singer Billie Holiday singing the words to the song "Strange Fruit." Abel Meeropol wrote the song in response to the 1930 lynching of Thomas Shipp and Abram Smith. *La Chingada* is not simply in the past; it is present. Jung (1969), in *Aion*, writes, "Today as never before it is important that human beings should not overlook the danger of the evil lurking within them" (p. 53).

Two Martyrs

There is another parallel in this archetypal moment as both martyrs are youthful and children of the divine. Jesus Christ is the son of God who dwells in heaven above, and Cuauhtémoc is the son of the earth goddess Coatlicue. These two martyrs are victims of fate: Christ's fate is crucifixion on the cross, and Cuauhtémoc's fate lies in the wind of prophecy. While the Mexica under Cuauhtémoc fought bravely, there was still a sacred world whose fall had been foretold by the ancient books of memory. "Prepare yourself, oh my little brothers, for the white twin of heaven has come, and he will castrate the sun, bringing night, and sadness, and the weight of pain." Such was the prophecy to be found in the Maya *Chilam Balam*, a codex formed of mystical texts, chronologies, and prophecies attributed to the priest Chilam Balam (Fuentes, 1992, p. 114).

The wounds of Christ and those of Cuauhtémoc are inflicted by their malevolent and bloodthirsty oppressors; both are taken prisoners. In the final moments, Christ cries out to his father. Cuauhtémoc, as Mexico's sacrificed son, remains silent, alone, and disconnected from the sanctity of Mexico. Cuauhtémoc is remembered not only as the last *tlatoani* of the Mexica but for his brutal death at the hands of Cortés. The psychological trauma goes beyond a simple comparison with Christ; it defines our very existence.

The Third

The year 2021 marked 500 years since the fall of the Tenochtitlán. Those events which occurred in Mexico City continue to haunt the Mexican and, unlike Sevilla in 1992, are remembered with profound sorrow. The Mexican and Chicanx not only recall the final moments of Christ and Cuauhtémoc but identify with the crucifixion and the martyrdom of both, which brought forth the birth of the *Mestizo*. This conception occurred alongside the viciousness of the Spanish Conquest. The union of the Spanish father and the indigenous mother occurred in the shadow of vicious ruthlessness. It reveals the duality of the Mexico-Chicanx soul, one conceived amid the ruins of the Mexica world. From the ashes of Conquest arose the *Mestizo* as the third. Carlos Fuentes (1992) writes about the birth of the *Mestizo*:

> We have a terrible knowledge, that of being present at the instance of our own creation, the observers of our own rape but also of the contrary contradictory cruelties and tenderness that went with our conception. Spanish Americans cannot be understood without acknowledgment meant of this intense consciousness of the moment in which we were conceived, children of a nameless mother, we ourselves anonymous, but fully aware of our father's name. A sort of magnificent pain welds together Iberia and the New World; a birth occurs along with the knowledge of all that had to die so that we should be born: the splendor of the ancient Indian civilization.
>
> (p. 16)

The heartbreaking impact of this genocide has never been fully explored from a depth psychological perspective. Cuauhtémoc's barbarous and brutal death reveals a cultural complex deeply rooted in the psyche of the Americas. The martyrdom of Cuauhtémoc is symbolic of our collective humiliation. Luigi Zoja (as cited in Singer, 2004) writes that the "activation of psychic layers are neither personal nor cultural but archetypal. In turn, the archetypal pattern may well express itself in a cultural complex or a personal complex or both" (p. 86).

The Resurrection

During *Semana Santa*, the week leading into Easter Sunday, the crucifixion is reenacted. I have seen men as they cut themselves with glass embedded in stone, others self-flagellate, while other men walk barefoot in chains. On Good Friday, in my community and in Spain, I witnessed the reenactment of the Stations of the Cross, which included a *penitente* portraying Christ's suffering as he carries a cross through the streets. I would argue that the *Mestizo* has been nailed to the cross for the last 500 years. Despite the suffering of the Conquest, the archetype of Jesus Christ and Cuauhtémoc are both images of transcendence. However, there is one decisive and fundamental difference: Jesus Christ transcends his earthly body and has resurrected. Cuauhtémoc has not. Cuauhtémoc, *the eagle that falls*, is buried in the depth of the Mayan forest, and the gravesite of his mutilated body remains a mystery. Paz (1962) explains the importance of this metaphorical event:

> Another element enters here, an analogy that makes this history a true poem in search of fulfillment: the location of Cuauhtémoc is unknown. The mystery of his burial site is one of our obsessions. To discover it would mean nothing less than to return to our origins, to reunite ourselves with our ancestors, to break out of our solitude. It would be a resurrection.
>
> (p. 84)

Ultimately, Cuauhtémoc is a mythical figure that represents our earthly and heavenly soul. His nameless burial site, his anonymity, has become characteristic of our "otherness," the unknown and the unseen.

The Lament

The Conquest of Mexico has brought forth a lament and yearning for the mythical. Hillman (1977) wrote that "mythical consciousness is a mode of being in the world that brings with it the imaginal person" (p. 17). The Mestizo desires a return to the gods and myths that speak to us and through us. This imaginal person is experienced in the divine image of La Llorona, also known to the Mexica as Cihuacoatl, the goddess of fertility. Cihuacoatl is also reported to have said before the arrival of Cortés, "O my children, you are lost, where shall I hide you?"

Her grief is now heard in the refrain, "*Mis hijos, donde estan mis hijos?* Under the monstrous shadow of the conquest, she can be heard wailing for those who have died and those who are lost. La Llorona cries for the Other. Her salted tears cry in anguish for the violent lynching of Mexicans, which began shortly after the Texas War of Independence and lasted for nearly a century, and today La Llorona wails in despair at the shores of the Rio Grande for migrant families separated and their lost children. She also moans for the brutality of slavery and the genocide of the Indigenous. La Llorona also weeps for the displacement of African Americans, victims of lynching, torture, and discrimination. La Llorona is the messenger who will not let us forget the atrocities and inequities of the past and those of today. "*Aye de mi Llorona, Llorona de ayer y hoy.*"

To live the symbolic life means not only to honor the traditions and cultures of all people but also to acknowledge and come to terms with the European shadow of colonialism. This is our "divine drama" (Jung, 1951). The mythology of Cuauhtémoc demands that we remember that which cannot be forgotten. Hillman (1977, p. 170) reminds us that the "Gods are never dead." The clash between the mythical world of pre-Columbian America and that of the Christian-Cartesian is with us today. In Los Angeles, in June of 2020, the statue of Franciscan priest Junipero Serra was toppled amid the burning of sage, drumming, and invocation to the ancestors. Latinx community activists and indigenous elders had gathered at *La Placita*, the city's birthplace, demanding that the story of the California mission system, which includes forced acculturation and brutal forced labor, be reframed to reflect the reality of *La Chingada*. As the statue was brought down, one could hear a woman shout, "This is for our ancestors!" (Figure 5.3). Conversely, it must be added that the Chingada Complex is everyone's complex:

Through scientific understanding, our world has become dehumanized. Man feels himself isolated in the cosmos. He is no longer involved in

Figure 5.3 Photo from L.A. Times, June 23, 2020

nature and has lost his emotional participation in natural events, which heretofore had a symbolic meaning for him. Thunder is no longer the voice of a god, nor is lightning his avenging missile. No river contains a spirit, or tree means a man's life, no snake is the embodiment of wisdom, and no mountain still harbors a great demon. Neither do things speak to him nor can he speak to things, like stones, springs, plants, and animals. He no longer has a bush-soul identifying him with a wild animal. His immediate communication with nature is gone forever, and the emotional energy it generates has sunk into the unconscious.

(Jung, 2012, p. 255)

Today there is a heavy sickness, and we are witnesses to this sickness, in the form of a worldwide pandemic, global warming, racism, and a world sharply divided between those of material privilege and those who have nothing. Psyche is demanding that we find a third way. Jung (1969) famously wrote in *Symbols of Transformation*, "Everyone knows nowadays that people have complexes. What is not so well known, though far more important theoretically, is that complexes can have us" (p. 96). By examining the violent legacy of the Conquest, we can begin to realize that the Chingada Complex has had us all, for not to do so is to remain unconscious to the necessity of resurrection.

References

de la O, J. (2020). An exploration of the Chingada complex: The legacy of conquest. *Psychological Perspectives*, *63*(3–4): 425–440. https://doi.org/10.1080/00332925.2020.1816082

Fehrenbach, T. R. (1995). *Fire & blood: A history of Mexico* (1st Da Capo Press ed. Updated). Da Capo Press.

Fuentes, C. (1992). *The buried mirror: Reflections on Spain and the new world*. Houghton Mifflin Harcourt.

Galeano, E., & Belfrage, C. (1985/1988). *Memory of fire* (1st American). Pantheon Books.

Golio, G. (2017). *Strange fruit: Billie Holiday and the power of a protest song*. Millbrook Press.

Gudait, G. I., & Stein, M. (2014). *Confronting cultural trauma: Jungian approaches to understanding and healing*. Spring Journal.

Hillman, J. (1977). *Re-visioning psychology*. HarperCollins.

Jung, C. G. (1951). *Collected works of C.G. Jung, volume 18: The symbolic life*. Princeton University Press.

Jung, C. G. (1961). *Collected works of C.G. Jung, volume 4: Freud & psychoanalysis*. Princeton University Press.

Jung, C. G. (1969a). *Collected works of C.G. Jung, volume 8: Symbols of transformation*. Routledge.

Jung, C. G. (1969b). *Collected works of C.G. Jung, volume 9ii: Aion*. Princeton University Press.

Jung, C. G. (1978). *C.G. Jung speaking*.

Jung, C. G. (2011). *Memories, dreams, reflections*. Vintage.

Jung, C. G. (2012). *Man and his symbols*. Dell.

Kimbles, S. L. (2021). *Intergenerational complexes in analytical psychology: The suffering of ghosts*. Routledge.

Maestri, N. (2019). *Connecting the upper, middle, and lower Maya realms*. ThoughtCo. www.thoughtco.com/ceiba-pentandra-sacred-tree-maya-171615

Meerpol, A. (1939). Strange fruit [Song]. In *Classics in swing*. Commodore.

Paz, O. (1962). *The labyrinth of solitude: Life and thought in Mexico*. Grove/Atlantic.

Singer, T., & Kimbles, S. L. (2004). *The cultural complex: Contemporary Jungian perspectives on psyche and society*. Routledge.

Tarnas, R. (2011). *The passion of the western mind*. Ballantine Books.

Chapter 6

America

The Gun

Randi Nathenson

On April 20, 1999, Dylan Klebold and Eric Harris went on a shooting spree at Columbine High School in Littleton, Colorado, killing thirteen people and wounding 20 before turning their guns on themselves. The massacre was premeditated and strategically planned, which is typical of mass shootings; they are not impulsive acts of rage (Duwe, 2000, 2004). Mass shootings hold an extensive and dark history in the United States, dating back to the 1700s, but it was Columbine which turned our national attention to these tragedies.

Since Columbine, these events have continued to occur, their names—Sandy Hook, Pulse Night Club, Virginia Tech, and so on—common in our vernacular. Mass shootings are the least common form of gun violence (Duwe, 2000), but they garner the greatest amount of attention, with little to no political action in the aftermath. What typically follows a mass shooting is a temporary increase in the push for gun control, public outcry, and increased security. Gun control advocates blame guns, violent video games, and bullies, whereas gun rights advocates blame the parents and declining moral values. Both sides strive to find a scapegoat on which to project their personal and collective shadow. The assumption is that naming a cause will solve the problem. This quick-fix cause-and-effect thinking is emblematic of American culture, which focuses on symptom eradication, rather than the *telos* of such events. What is ignored is our own violent nature: in essence, the mass shooter in each of us. The symbolic nature of the gun, which is central to our cultural identity, is also ignored rather than integrated.

Amid the finger-pointing after each mass shooting, few ask the harder questions; there is little deeper reflection. There is no inner soul searching. We remain stunned and unconscious. Mass shootings reflect our collective and individual shadow, a symptom of a deeper and darker problem that

DOI: 10.4324/9781003252993-7

extends beyond the need for gun control and scapegoats. While common-sense gun control measures are needed, background checks and weapon bans are not likely to stop mass murder. Violence is inherent to the human experience. As Jungian analyst Luigi Zoja (2009) stated, "To imagine that violence can be done away with is a risky over-simplification. The great-est atrocities of the past have been predicated on the denial of violence as natural or inherently human" (p. 4).

Gun Symbolism and American Gun Culture

Paradoxically, the gun is imbued with a multiplicity of uses. It carries with it the capability of both life and death. The gun can be used for hunting, protection, defense, and as a weapon. The gun can provide food for one's family or be used to commit atrocities against one's family. This paradox is described in *The Book of Symbols:*

> The gun plays an ambivalent role in the history of human survival and human carnage; hunting for food can be set alongside the extinction of entire animal species; the protection of home and hearth can be weighed against our staggering murder rates.
>
> (ARAS, 2010, p. 498)

The etymology of the word *gun* is derived from the Scandinavian *Gunhildr*, which means battle-maiden. Gunhildr was a quasi-historical figure known for her cruelty and violence. Thus, the gun is personified, transformed from an inanimate but deadly hunk of metal and plastic into a powerful, enlivened character. The word *gun* is heavily interspersed in the images of everyday language; in idiom and metaphor, we speak of jumping the gun, being quick on the draw, and trigger-happy, the gun becomes as a represen-tation of power, rage, aggression, strength, impulsivity, speed, carelessness, and decisiveness, to name a few.

The gun is thought of as a phallic symbol, and the pleasure derived from shooting guns is often described as erotic; the gun connects the shooter to both generative and destructive instincts—power, sex, death, and life in one seemingly simple apparatus. There is an erotic element to mass shoot-ings, perhaps a grandiose and perverted display of one's phallic power, or an extreme compensation of an inner experience of powerlessness and rejection.

Hillman refers to the gun as a Hephaestion instrument that allows us to "hold the gods in our hand, carry death in your purse" (p. 124). He states that the gun is

> a fearful thing of beauty that holds Ares, Aphrodite, and Hephaistos all together in a fine piece of metalwork. . . . Human beings love their weapons, crafting them with the skill of Hephaistos, and the beauty of Aphrodite, for the purposes of Ares.
>
> (p. 124)

The gun becomes a container for archetypal energies, allowing us to possess this power, to become like gods ourselves, thereby concretizing the symbolic.

The United States has a unique gun culture which differentiates us from other countries, adding complexity and nuance to the symbolic significance as well as the conversation around mass shootings. The United States is one of three countries where gun ownership is afforded by the constitution (Waldman, 2014); the Second Amendment has become an almost religious doctrine that reinforces the importance of guns in our culture.

Guns were significant in the formation of the United States, helping us to win the Revolutionary War, granting us the power to massacre Native Americans in the expansion of our conquered territory under the ideology of Manifest Destiny (Hofstadter, 1970). Guns remain an icon, an archetypal image of the country that has come to embody what is sacred to Americans: individualism, freedom, rights, and power. If our origin myth centers around the gun, the gun then becomes sacred, and what follows is resistance to removing guns from their pedestal.

Robert Jay Lifton has argued that American gun culture is different than that of other countries because we lack a traditional base:

> America has been built on continuous immigration and patterns of movement. We also didn't start with a traditional culture in place; maybe no country does, but we had even less of one to begin with. In America all sorts of cultures have come together to form the concept of "the American." But our *identity* has always been shaky; we've always been uneasy about our lack of a longer history or a traditional culture. Sometimes that uneasiness has made us emphasize what history we do have all the more strongly. . . . As a country we tend to look for ways to compensate for

the absence of a traditional cultural base. And in my view the identity we've built around conquering the wilderness, the gun, and our constitutional right to self-defense together form a major compensation for that absence of tradition.

(as cited in Peay, 2005)

Guns are connected to the American dream, which is focused on achievement, success, and material desires. Symbolically, the American dream reinforces the cultural ethos of Manifest Destiny and westward movement, of settling the frontier, and the gun provides us with the means to do so and a potential solution when we cannot. The inability to fulfill what is dictated by the American dream can lead one to feel like a failure, full of shame, and worthless. These feelings and experiences are common, and typical of people who enter my consulting room. Often people come to therapy questioning their lives, their paths, and their purpose. Underneath these emotions may be feelings of anger or rage, of feeling devalued and disempowered. The work of analysis is often to increase one's consciousness of these feelings and the ways in which they manifest.

In his essay "A Psychology of Bullets," Glen Slater (2000) explores gun violence as the shadow side of the cultural expectations of the American dream. Slater examines our obsession with the idea that everyone could (and should) rise up and become something, preferably wealthy and successful, valuing materialism above all else. Slater states that "beneath the cloak of normative goals and aspirations, we have fervently embraced a cluster of social values that can be identified as precursors of gun violence" (p. 20). The inability to fulfill this dream constellates an affective experience including a sense of rejection, alienation, and anger, necessitating a corrective response that can turn violent:

The gun appears when the gap between actual life and the idealized American Dream opens too wide; the gun is fired when there is no *thing* left to satisfy the belief that we make our own destiny . . . the role of the gun is to extend and protect willful intent when self-image and personal goals are threatened.

(p. 21)

In the absence of achievement, the gun becomes a validation.

While there is no common profile for a mass shooter, a typical character-istic of mass shooters is that they tend to feel rejected, alienated, and cut off from society. Shootings are often experienced as a manner to reclaim some lost sense of power. The gun provides us with the means to achieve, and a potential solution when we cannot.

Mass shooting cannot simply be reduced to the proliferation of guns or our gun culture. Nor can it be reduced to any of the other common scape-goats such as bullying, mental health, videogames, or moral decline. The problem is larger and more complex.

Mass shootings are most frequently perpetrated by white males, but just as this is not simply an issue of guns, this is not merely an issue of white maleness. The reasons for this trend have more to do with socialization than physiology, a result of patriarchy, privilege, toxic masculinity, gen-der stereotypes, and racial bias. While aggression is encouraged and even rewarded in white males, in females, and particularly in females of color along with non-white males, the expression of aggression and rage tends to be viewed pathologically, judged more harshly, and discouraged. The ques-tion is not what is innate in white men, but how our culture promotes this violence by them.

Recent mass shootings in Atlanta, Charleston, and Pittsburgh demon-strate the connection of mass shootings to racism, misogyny, homophobia, and anti-Semitism. This highlights the connection of the gun to the main-tenance of oppressive power structures. The history of guns in America, as well as the history of gun control, is also a history that is inexorably linked with systematic racism and sexism. As a symbol of power, the gun has become caught up in the struggle to harness and maintain power, and who has access to that power has typically been controlled and decided by white men.

Gun control laws have historically been enacted as ways to bar people of color from buying guns. This was, in fact, one of the original goals of the KKK (Winkler, 2013). In the 1970s, the NRA turned from being a non-partisan group that supported gun control to the extreme right-wing animal it is today, in part, in response to the Civil Rights Movement. Gun rights became a political rallying cry that could run counter to freedom marches, as Burbick (2006) asserts: "Individual ownership of weapons became the foundation of freedom and as a result conveniently countered the collec-tive nonviolent political language of civil rights" (p. 91). Indeed, the NRA continues to be the spokesperson for white power and for the expression of white men to maintain that power through holding onto their guns.

Gun Complex

After each mass shooting, Americans collectively enter a brief period of mourning, offer up thoughts and prayers, engage in a great deal of finger-pointing, take part in debates around Second Amendment rights, call for increased mental health services, push toward gun control legislation—and offer more thoughts and prayers. The attention each mass shooting garners is short-lived, and the response rarely goes beyond the surface, prompting no change or reflection. Proposed interventions fail to come to fruition. It is a predictable story on constant repeat. The difficulty we seem to have with reflecting and enacting change is, in part, a symptom of a personal and cultural gun complex.

The gun complex helps to keep us stuck in the gridlock of the gun debate. Each mass shooting repeatedly reignites the debate about guns in America. The gun debate is emotional, affect-ridden, and extremely polarized, often along political party lines. The two sides refuse to listen to one another or compromise, seeing the other as wrong. Any legislation is met with a zealous complex ridden response. The gun debate creates a false dichotomy, an either/or mindset:

> The two groups compete with each other for political and social resources . . . each of these groups considers itself part of the mainstream of the broader American culture while at the same time portraying the other as participating in a separate and irrational subculture.
>
> (Utter and True, 2000, p. 67)

The two sides refuse to listen to one another, instead engaging in projection, seeing the other as corrupt, imprudent, and irresponsible. From the stance of gun rights advocates, gun control advocates are naive, dishonest, power-hungry, and irrationally afraid of guns. Gun rights advocates negate and minimize our aggression, our rage, and our power, and refuse to recognize the positive potential of the conscious integration of this symbolic material. The gun control side sees gun rights advocates as paranoid, uneducated, regressive, power-hungry, dishonest about guns, and profit-hungry.

The strongest and most powerful voice in the debate is that of the National Rifle Association, which is essentially a de facto trade association that is the primary lobbying group for the gun manufacturing industry. The NRA and the gun manufacturers are in a symbiotic relationship, and they both benefit when guns become a political issue. For the NRA, it's about members and money. "For the gun manufacturers, it's about sales and protection from legal liability. And as long as gun owners are kept agitated, angry, and afraid, they both win" (Waldman, 2016). The rhetoric suggests that members of the NRA expect another American Revolution any minute, that they will again need to take up arms against a tyrannical government that threatens their freedoms. Somehow any background check or waiting period is perceived as a threat, a slippery slope to a dictatorship, and the demise of individual liberty. The NRA lobbies hard and works to convince gun owners that liberals aspire to take their guns away, which serves to increase gun sales.

The right to bear arms has become more than a right to own a weapon and protect oneself; it has become a larger phenomenon constellated around the gun complex. Within the complex, there is an archetypal possession, an identification with the archetype in which shadow parts of oneself become projected onto the gun. Instead of being a symbol, the archetype of the gun becomes literalized and concrete. The gun becomes an identity, a solution, a way of maintaining one's sense of power and agency. The shadow of this is the gun's destructive potential. Within this complex, the shadow remains unconscious and projected outward. Both the gun rights and gun control sides of the debate remain unconscious; the complex is either identified with or unintegrated.

In *Kinds of Power: A Guide to Its Intelligent Uses*, Hillman (1995) argued that the love of guns may not be so much about violence as about fear of being violated and losing one's power:

> Since the god is in the gun, the passionate love for these weapons may express less a love of violence than a magical protection against it. [The gun becomes] a fetish or amulet to hold at bay the fear of injury or death . . . a charm against the paranoid anxieties that haunt the American psyche.
>
> (p. 127)

Americans do not want to give up their gods. The NRA member's paranoid fear of being disarmed, the belief that liberals are "coming for your guns," reflects an identification with this archetypal terror that one's very being is threatened. The gun allows Ares energy to become available, as Hillman (1995) stated: "The automatic in my hand brings Mars to my side" (p. 128). In Hillman's reference, Mars is the Roman version of the Greek Ares.

This militaristic and frontier mentality remains in our collective psyche. The language of gun rights advocates often echoes this mentality, speaking of the need to protect and defend themselves. There is a sense of a continual readiness for revolution, the need to take up arms against a tyrannical government at any moment.

The archetypal image of the gun, and its utilization for power, solving problems, channeling aggression and rage, and finding justice are just a few motifs that surround gun culture and appear in widely American TV shows, movies, books, art, and video games. We see this in the various *Star Wars* movies, *James Bond* films, comic books, action movies, and stories of superheroes.

The gun debate exemplifies how, while the United States values unity, not division, we are extremely polarized. Zoja states that "this culture of unity at all costs has transformed itself into a one-sided negation of shadow, that is to say, of divisiveness or divisions which are an ordinary human reality" (Zoja, 2009, p. 14). Rather than allow for tension and splitting, we instead insist on consensus, which permits no space for reflection, conversation, debate, and discussion. Rather than engage with curiosity, the complex remains rigid and intractable. Zoja (2009) states, "If consciousness accepts only one aspect of a polarity the other aspect sets up a clamor in the unconscious until repression no longer works and there is some kind of explosion" (p. 14).

These hostile and unnuanced stances within the collective might be understood by recognizing America's relative youth and immaturity as a country. Our gun culture is regressed because American culture remains underdeveloped. An undeveloped psyche can stand behind—or against—the gun as the solution to our problems. This is a space where the political and the psychological become linked, where the gun's symbolic place in the American psyche holds enormous influence over politics. In our culture, the absence of individual reflection leads to an overidentification with the gun and its collective meaning. In order to both personally and collectively individuate, we must separate our current identity from the past and be conscious of our heritage, but not identify with it. Roy (2004) warned, "When identification with an archetype takes place, a normal ego loses its bearing, is overwhelmed, and may even face a psychotic breakdown" (p. 71). Our cultural identification with the gun as sacred casts a shadow by (or on the basis of) which mass shootings have become the extremely destructive way of assimilating that power.

A mass shooting represents the destructive nature of the complex, the dark side of holding the gun as a sacred and archetypal object. The shooting is a way of maintaining and adhering to one's power. When stuck in energy that supports and encourages taking up arms as a solution to problems, the mass shooting becomes a viable resolution, a way in which power can be reclaimed and one can assert oneself, be heard, and be seen. What gets projected outward is the need to destroy, to annihilate, in order to support the ego position. I wonder if what is happening *symbolically* in the mass shooting is that the shooter has become caught up in an enactment of the complex, possessed by the archetypal energy of the gun.

Unconscious of this destructive and violent shadow and identified with the gun complex, we are collectively possessed by the archetypal energy of Ares, which we either repress, enact, or collude with. What is required is a more reflective stance where we can ruminate on and integrate these parts. Again, complexes cannot be gotten rid of; what we can do is depotentiate their energy to minimize the impact and hold they have over us. Developing an understanding of the American gun complex provides a way to explore why mass shootings are an American phenomenon.

The Ares Archetype

While other archetypal energies are at play—in the strategic planning of the shootings, in the amassing of arms needed, and so on—it is Ares who drew me in. The archetype of Ares is an image of life that is uncontained, destructive, chaotic, and violent. Although this brutal and caustic force can be found in other mythological figures, I was struck by his story. Ares is neither a proud warrior god nor a vengeful authoritarian deity. He is depicted as the rejected child of Zeus and Hera. The name *Ares* comes from the Greek word for "ruin" or "curse." His epithets include "killer of men," "destroyer," and "murderer." Ares does not have the revered all-powerful authority of Zeus who throws thunderbolts at whoever crosses him, nor does he possess the wisdom and strategy of Athena on the battlefield. Ares is despised by most immortals and experiences frequent humiliation both on and off the battlefield. Ares is not so much the god of war as the personification of the horrors of it. He is father to Phobos and Deimos, fear and panic. Ares revels in the violence, not needing a reason for it, interested in annihilation, rather than motivated by a particular cause. The violence of Ares is violence that comes from a dark, wounded place, a raging response to injustice, rejection, and isolation, violence for the sake of revenge whether the circumstances demand it or not. It is a desire to reclaim power one feels they have lost, or never had, or feels that one deserves.

In art, he is often depicted in full body armor, carrying a shield and spear. His home is in the wild, barbarous land of Thrace; the psychological landscape of Ares is a space that can feel affectively unbearable. I wonder if a mass shooting is both this repulsive space and the result of being situated psychologically within in it.

Ares is the action that occurs on the battlefield. With the gun, the shooter can evoke the nature of Ares; he has the ability to destroy masses with a hunk of metal and plastic. The mass shooting becomes an extreme way to reclaim one's power, to make oneself known and infamous, and, thereby, to reclaim what they believe is owed to them. The mass shooter is archetypally possessed, caught in an inflated state; pulling the trigger sweeps the shooter into a reality that transcends human potential and allows for revenge, and for retribution. The myth of Ares gets played out in destructive fashion.

Ares, known for his beauty, figures often in stories of affairs, particularly with Aphrodite. While this pairing may seem paradoxical, it speaks to psychological balance and conscious integration of one's destructive capacity. Harmonia and Eros are born from this union, speaking to conscious integration, and the creative potential of Ares, rather than an identification with or revulsion towards it. Having access to these energies also allows us to access our creative instincts. Jung refers to the process of individuation as a creative process, requiring work and conscious energy. In a letter written in 1932, Jung wrote, "The best way for dealing with the unconscious is the creative way" (1973, p. 109). Creativity can act as a constructive way of making sense of the inner chaos, of integrating our rage and our aggression and our desire for violence. Diamond (1996) referred to creativity as the "constructive utilization of the daimonic" (p. 256), which gives structure to the darkness and chaos. If the positive potential of aggression, rage, and power is my own creativity, then "anger and rage can be an enlivening, transformative, creative, even spiritual force" (Diamond, 1996, p. 13).

In the *Idea of the Holy*, Rudolf Otto (1950) explores the experience of the numinous, to which he refers as the feeling of the "*mysterium tremendum*," an overwhelmingly powerful experience. Otto (1950) states that this feeling has the potential to be wonderful, but that it also has "wild and demonic forms and can sink to an almost grisly horror and shuddering" (p. 13). This speaks to the creative and destructive potential of Ares. When constellated, the image can pair with the love and beauty of Aphrodite or the wisdom of Athena, or it can unleash the horror of the mass shooting. It is a psychotic place where strangers become one's abusers, those against whom you have to seek revenge. There is a rush of adrenaline and, yes, joy in the idea of taking up a gun and shooting, unleashing destruction and chaos. It is a place of wanting to be heard and seen. It refuses to be silent; it is as loud as possible.

Guns in the Consulting Room

Our cultural complex around guns is also a personal one that plays out in our consulting rooms. Rage, anger, and aggression are often experiences with which analysands struggle in integrating the Ares energy, or what I term "the inner gun." These affects enter our consulting rooms often, many times unconsciously, defensively, complex-ridden, and unintegrated. At times these energies are directed outward, while at other times inward. Edinger (1972) described suicidal and homicidal tendencies as being opposite sides of the same experience of rejection and alienation, a rupture in the ego-self axis. One's response can be rage, turned both inward and outward.

Conscious connection to this power, to our own aggression and rage, gives us access to our inner gun; in this way, we have agency and control over it; we can ensure that we don't simply "go off" or explode like "loose cannons." There are times when we need access to this energy, to use our gun—our inner power—to protect ourselves or others from harm, to stand up for ourselves, or, at times, to complete tasks. The inner gun symbolizes our capacity to maintain our sense of self, staying grounded in our center.

In his books *Human Aggression* (1995) and *Human Destructiveness* (1991), Anthony Storr explores the nature of aggression, supporting the claim that there are positive and negative features to aggression, that it is, in fact, instinctive and needed: "Aggression seems clearly linked with self-preservation, self-assertion, and self-affirmation" (Storr, 1991, p. 7). Aggression is also connected to defending oneself and asserting one's identity. Aggression allows for intentionality; it can drive behavior in a situation in which there is conflict or competition. Having safe and conscious access to one's aggression requires a sense of one's worth.

Rage in and of itself is neither positive nor negative; it is what one does with the rage that can be problematic. When unmediated or unconscious, it has destructive potential. All of us must get in touch with our rage and find ways to channel it. Jan Weiner (1998) talks about rage as holding more intensity than anger; anger is more controlled, less fiery, whereas rage implies a loss of control. Rage is hot, elemental, primitive, unpredictable, dangerous, and connected to shame. According to Weiner (1998), anger is more related to the ego as it has a cognitive component and is, to a point, controllable, whereas rage bypasses the ego and comes from the Self. Jung (1960) posited, "When we are beside ourselves with rage, we are obviously no longer identical with ourselves but are possessed by a demon or spirit" (CW 8, paras. 6). Rage emerges when someone's security is threatened, when there are injuries to self-esteem or pride, or when someone feels ridiculed, humiliated, or ignored. Reacting with rage to these injuries can be a regulator, proof that you know you have worth, value, and integrity. It is saying that you cannot do this to me or treat me this way. Anger and rage can be adaptive in response to a threat.

When anger and rage are unchecked, they can have destructive and negative impacts. The problem is "too much socially sanctioned self-suppression . . . [where] anger and resentment build over time into a morbidly murderous rage" (Diamond, 1996, p. 13). In these cases, "our unresolved resentment, anger, and rage has turned violent, toxic, cancerous" (Diamond, 1996, p. 20). I believe, as Diamond has asserted, that "most of us have been culturally conditioned to suppress our rebellious anger and rage, taught that we have no right to be irate about our state, that we stoically ought not cry out against our often-outrageous fate" (p. 26).

What follows are two clinical vignettes which describe this.

Kara

Kara is a 48-year-old woman who came to analysis cut off from her anger and caught in a complex around her aggression, rage, and power, that made her seem quite small and very young. Her mother's emotional absence and her father's explosive and violent nature had left her with a sense of loneliness, insecurity, and isolation, for which she compensated by maintaining her persona as mother, wife, and nurse, doing what she could to function within her very busy life.

When Kara entered analysis, she held the belief that any expression of anger was inherently wrong. She came to therapy depressed and anxious, in part due to her shadow material, which was linked to her father complex. Her father carried the Ares energy in the most destructive of ways, and this overwhelmed and terrified Kara. Her own rejected and unintegrated Ares energy was turned inward, in a self-destructive manner through alcoholism, anorexia, and self-harm. In this way, her rage was repressed and inaccessible. Kara would express that she did not want to be angry, that to be angry was to be her father, and she did not want to be him.

Within the analytic shadow work, when these defensive structures were challenged, Kara would become overwhelmed and anxious. She would tear up and have difficulty speaking, appearing physically smaller than she was. I often had the image of Lily Tomlin from the TV show *Laugh In* when she played Edith Ann, sitting in a giant rocking chair. When in this space, I felt as if I were talking to a small child who was afraid and vulnerable. Kara lacked any connection to an "inner gun"; her Ares energy was trapped. Graves (1955) told of a myth in the *Iliad* wherein Ares is kidnapped by two chthonic giants who trap him in an urn. He remains there for 13 months, a lunar year. Hermes and Artemis rescue him by tricking the giants into killing each other. This speaks to Kara's psychological experience of her Ares being trapped in an urn, dead, unreachable, and relegated to shadow. Much of our work has been to develop a connection with this part of herself, which has been a slow process.

As Kara and I worked together, we have focused on developing a more conscious connection to her anger, which has allowed her to connect to her own darkness. We used her dreams and active imaginations in which she would dialogue with her inner child, connecting to this part which was afraid and unheard. For Kara, the work was to creatively channel aggression and rage in order to access her inner sense of power. In becoming more creative in her inner world, she could grow in her outer world.

Two years into the work, Kara brought this dream to analysis:

I am in a child's room. I am looking around the room and observing it. There are no children in the room. I look down and I realize that in my hand I am holding a gun.

As we walked around this dream, it initially made Kara anxious; the concept of the gun overwhelmed her and constellated her complex. As we explored these feelings, there was a deeper recognition of her own power, her own anger, and a conscious stance from where she could enter her painful childhood material without regression, fear, and self-destruction.

Kara's shadow work allowed her to fantasize about rage, which led to a movement from victim to her own inner Ares, integrating the gun she held in her hand. She became the aggressor rather than the powerless. The fantasy became an image that reflected a possibility, an image to which we would continually return, where she could connect to her own power.

Amanda

Amanda is a 59-year-old woman whose analysis started with rage; Ares entered the room almost immediately, wild and untethered. She did not trust easily and quickly dismissed friends or family members when she felt slighted, used, or rejected. She would explode into rages, often directed at her husband. In this humiliated and rejected place, Ares was constellated, and her response within this Ares energy was to wipe out anyone she perceived had wronged her.

Amanda's chaotic upbringing was framed by abuse and neglect, in the context of which she experienced frequent humiliation, upheaval, and rejection. Her response to this was rage. In her rages, she became furious, unconsciously projecting the negligent parent who could not support or take care of her onto whatever hook she could find. There was a talion response, a desire for revenge.

She brought this dream:

> I am at my house where I grew up, and I am in the back where there is this deck; it wasn't there when I was a child. I am looking at the sky, and there are thunder clouds and lightning. Then I look out, and there are these storm troopers running through the backyard with guns, shooting people. They are all screaming.

We saw this dream as an image of being able to observe and explore the destructive rage within her, in order to consciously integrate these feelings. The situation was highly threatening, highlighting the need for conscious access to Ares, her inner gun, rather than her current relationship wherein she would routinely "go off" or express her rage in an unfiltered form. She required containment and an ability for discernment; I wondered whether an aspect of what she needed was the urn, a place where she could safely store Ares until needed.

Within the work, we explored what triggered her explosions in order to understand the telos of her anger (or complex). What was being expressed in psyche? I would carefully challenge her projections, wondering what was happening in her, connecting her to her feelings.

Amanda often became angry at me, perceiving me as the negative and uncaring mother who could not attend to or soothe her. She experienced me, at times, as having betrayed her. In such instances, her gun was drawn, and Ares was in the room, filled with rage and out for revenge. This was an excruciating experience for both of us. I had to resist an overly defensive or apologetic response, while at the same time holding a boundary. I held my inner gun to protect my sense of self, and she held hers, threatening to shoot. As she attempted to "shoot" me, I held the place where I wanted to shoot back. I found myself angry with her, wanting her to just "get over it and move on." I see this as perhaps a projective identification in which I took on the negative mother she was projecting onto me. From the strength of our relationship, we were able to work through this rage in the consulting room, processing it, looking at it, and coming to a place where neither of us were killed off. She became more related to Ares, to her own "mass shooter," so that she could integrate rather than lash out.

These two clinical vignettes both illustrate some of the different ways in which the inner gun may manifest and how it plays out within the analytic dyad. Kara was cut off from her own aggression and rage, expressing fear of it, worried that she would spiral out of control or fall to pieces. Amanda, on the other hand, would lash out, her inner Ares emerging in unconscious destructive ways. When rage is unconscious, it is dangerous and can result in individuals "venting their venomous hatred and rage on innocent bystanders" (Diamond, 1996, p. 27), as happens in a mass shooting. Recognizing and integrating aggression and rage are important parts of the individuation process in which we come to understand our potential for becoming the aggressor and find our connection to our own power. This shadow work is a crucial part of analytic work, and the inner gun can be seen as a symbol for the development of a conscious relationship to aggression, rage, and power, which are necessary to hold in consciousness.

Conclusion

As I traveled through the material, I came to understand mass shootings as a symptom of an American cultural complex around guns. Picking up a gun and shooting people has become a solution in a society that is hyper-focused on success and materialism. I call for deeper reflection that goes beyond the thoughts and prayers hashtag into understanding our own individual gun complex and how it leads to a resistance to true dialogue and common-sense gun control. As I mentioned, however, the problem of mass shootings extends far beyond gun control. In a sense, the debate on gun control is missing the point. On both an individual and community level, we must also work to develop a connection with our individual and collective shadow. It is in this reflection on our own destructive capabilities that we can gain insight into mass shootings and a deeper consciousness of the phenomenon. This requires a conscious integration of the archetypal nature of the gun, rather than an identification with or revulsion to it.

Having access to these energies also allows us to access our creative instincts. Jung refers to the process of individuation as a creative process, requiring work and conscious energy. As Jung (1966) has written, "the unsatisfied yearning of the artist reaches back to the primordial image in the unconscious which is best fitted to compensate for the inadequacy and one-sidedness of the present" (CW 15, para. 130).

References

Archive for Research in Archetypal Symbolism (ARAS). (2010). *The Book of Symbols: Reflections on Archetypal Images*. Cologne, Germany: Taschen.

Burbick, J. (2006). *Gun Show Nation: Gun Culture and American Democracy*. New York, NY: New Press.

Diamond, S. A. (1996). *Anger, Madness and the Daimonic: The Psychological Genesis of Violence, Evil, and Creativity*. Albany, NY: State University of New York Press.

Duwe, G. (2000). Body-count journalism: The presentation of mass murder in the news media. *Homicide Studies, 4*(4), 364–399.

Duwe, G. (2004). The patterns and prevalence of mass murder in twentieth-century America. *Justice Quarterly, 21*, 729–761.

Edinger, E. F. (1972). *Ego and Archetype: Individuation and the Religious Function of the Psyche*. Boston, MA: Shambhala.

Graves, R. (1955). *The Greek Myths*. London, England: Penguin Books.

Hillman, J. (1995). *Kinds of Power: A Guide to Its Intelligent Uses* (1st ed.). Currency Doubleday.

Hofstadter, R. (1970). America as a gun culture. *American Heritage*, *21*(6). Retrieved from www.americanheritage.com/content/america-gun-culture

Jung, C. G. (1960). *The Structure and Dynamics of the Psyche. Collected Works* (Vol. 8). New York, NY: Bollingen Series, Princeton University Press.

Jung, C. G. (1966). *The Practice of Psychotherapy. Collected Works* (Vol. 16). New York, NY: Bollingen Series, Princeton University Press.

Jung, C. G. (1973). *Letters (Vol. 1: 1906–1950)*. London, England: Routledge.

Otto, R. (1950). *The Idea of the Holy*. London, UK: Oxford University Press.

Peay, P. (2005, August 6). The gun, the bomb, and the wound that will not heal: An interview with Robert Jay Lifton. *Psychology Today*. Retrieved from www.psychologytoday.com/blog/america-the-couch/201508/the-gun-the-bomb-and-the-wound-will-not-heal

Roy, M. (2004). Religious archetype as cultural complex. In T. Singer & S. Kimbles (Eds.), *The Cultural Complex: Contemporary Jungian Perspectives on Psyche and Society* (pp. 64–77). New York, NY: Routledge.

Slater, G. (2000). A psychology of bullets: Gun violence and the American dream. *The Salt Journal*, *2*(1), 19–24.

Storr, A. (1991). *Human Destructiveness*. New York: Grove Press.

Storr, A. (1995). *Human Aggression*. New York, NY: Penguin.

Utter, G. H., & True, J. L. (2000). The evolving gun culture in America. *The Journal of American Culture*, *23*(2), 67–79. doi:10.1111/j.1542-734x.2000.2302_67.x

Waldman, M. (2014). *The Second Amendment: A Biography*. New York, NY: Simon & Schuster Paperbacks.

Waldman, P. (2016). How the NRA and gun manufacturers work together to scam gun owners. *The Week*. Retrieved from https://theweek.com/articles/597752/how-nra-gun-manufacturers-work-together-scam-gun-owners

Weiner, J. (1998). Under the volcano: Varieties of anger and their transformation. *Journal of Analytic Psychology*, *43*, 493–508.

Winkler, A. (2013). *Gunfight: The Battle Over the RIGHT to Bear Arms in America*. New York, NY: W. W. Norton & Co.

Zoja, L. (2009). *Violence in History, Culture, and Psyche: Essays*. New Orleans, LA: Spring Journal Books.

Chapter 7

An Ecological Future Beyond the Pandemic

Dennis Merritt

The mounting apocalyptic effects of climate change, the loss of biodiversity, the destruction of the planet's rain forests, the mining of soils vital for agriculture to produce 35% more food by 2050—the challenges are overwhelming. Many are calling this the Anthropocene Era—an era delineated by the effect of one species, humans, on the entire planet. It is essential that we analyze our dysfunctional relationship with the environment—and with each other—at the deepest levels before offering an archetypal framework for moving towards a sustainable future, a future that has been deeply compromised by human activities.

Carl Jung's psychology offers a conceptual system both broad and deep enough to embrace the dimensions of understanding and change necessary to meet these daunting challenges. Jung brings an archetypal perspective to ecopsychology—a new field that emerged in the 1990s to study our human relationship with the environment and develop ways to deepen our connection with nature. I am a lifelong environmentalist but did not fully realize the ecological scope of Jung's system until I neared completion of my efforts to integrate Jungian psychology, science, and Native American spirituality in my four volumes of *The Dairy Farmer's Guide to the Universe—Jung, Hermes, and Ecopsychology* (Merritt, 2012–2013). Jung predicted in 1940 that a necessary paradigm shift was coming in the West. His understanding of astrology led him to believe we were on the cusp of the Aquarian Age, what he also called a "new age" (Jung, 1973, p. 285). This new age is upon us. The COVID-19 pandemic has amplified the problems and inequalities in modern society and has put us in a position to entertain revolutionary ideas and make dramatic changes.

Ecology Begins in the Dreamworld

Ecology is the study of the movement of energy and matter between living forms and between those forms and their physical environment, revealing

DOI: 10.4324/9781003252993-8

intricate and complex patterns of relationships and interconnectedness. We must develop an ecological sense of the interconnectedness of everything that can be extended to our human relationships and the systems we establish. As Jungian analyst and imaginal psychologist James Hillman asserts, environmental pathologies make us aware that we are part of nature, because our actions affect the environment and make life difficult for everyone (Hillman, 1992, pp. 89–100). *Mitaquye Oyasin*, the Lakota Sioux say: "We are all related." This is a fundamental construct in ecopsychology, what I call the ecology of psychology and the psychology of ecology.

Missing from environmental movements is the intra-psychic dimension of the human experience. Ecology begins by recognizing the importance Jung gives to being in relationship to "the little people" within, the people in our dreams who are both part of ourselves (Gestalt therapy) and an aspect of the "Other," something bigger than the ego (CW8, par. 209). How we relate to our "inner tribe" (Internal Family Systems, Schwartz, 1997) is how we relate to those around us: "As above, so below; as within, so without," the alchemists proclaimed.

We become better citizens, "citizens of the cosmos," as Hillman suggests, when we develop a relationship to the unconscious (Hillman, 1988, pp. 62–63). According to Jung, you don't become enlightened by imagining figures of light, but by bringing as much light as possible to the unconscious (CW13, par. 335). If we are not conscious of our own dark side, our shadow, we project it onto other sexes, races, economic and ethnic groups, etc., discredit, and attack them. It is humbling to deal with the dark and seemingly unchangeable elements within ourselves, yet doing so prevents us from becoming self-righteous. We have greater compassion and understanding of others when we experience the lengthy, arduous task of changing things we don't like in ourselves. This is crucial at a political level where a democracy depends on an informed electorate, an openness to opposing positions, and a willingness to engage in dialogue.

The relationship between the ego and the unconscious is a fractal of the individual in relation to the collective, and humans in relation to the natural world. Jung's metaphor is that of a cell in the human body (Jung, 1997, pp. 753–754; Merritt, 2012, pp. 37–38). Basic metabolisms and functions occur within the cell just as an individual human functions within a society. The incredibly complex and intricate interactions of the cells must function perfectly for the individual human to be healthy. These are systems within systems, selves within selves in a Jungian sense, where no part can be isolated from the other, there are no dominant elements, and systems operate as an interactive whole to maintain the integrity of the organism.

Hillman's model for the human psyche is the ant's nest or beehive (Hillman, 1988, p. 59), which aligns with the scientific concept of organism that extends from the subatomic to the galactic, all operating on the mathematical principles of complexity theory—revolutionary concepts that began to emerge in the 1960s. We emotionally, metaphorically, and symbolically experience the working of complex systems when we have dreams wherein several "little people" interact with the dream ego, always within a particular setting and narrative.

We Have Become a Cancer on the Planet

Cancer occurs when cells develop out of relationship to larger systems and divert the body's resources for their own development. This form of disease is a good analogy for an ego out of relationship to the broader and unconscious whole—the Self from which it emerges—and for individuals who feel little sense of connection and responsibility to other humans. Such a dynamic has been painfully demonstrated by Americans who refused to wear masks or get vaccinated during the pandemic, claiming it would infringe on their individual freedom and rights. The archetypal core of this hyper-individualism is the romantic image of the cowboy in the American collective unconscious—a rugged, mythic figure in the wilds without any restrictions upon him. Politicians often manipulate this core by promoting a cowboy image of themselves and feeding a fear of socialism/communism and "Big Government."

The cancer metaphor can be extended to the human relationship to the planet in the form of the ultimate anti-ecological system—the corporate model that trumps national laws, human rights, and environmental standards. If a corporation were a person, as recognized by the Supreme Court's *Citizens United* decision, it would be the ultimate narcissist. Corporations strive to eliminate competition; their sole aim is to make money. People are expendable, and the environment is seen simply as a resource base and a waste dump.

Corporations "greenwash" their crimes through advertising and create a consumer culture consuming the planet as it stokes our individual narcissism. We are immersed from an early age in advertising that tells us we deserve it—*now*; this product will make us more attractive and superior;

that we can *literally* buy meaning and happiness. Hermes is the god of advertising, and his subtle and trickster ways are seen in pharmaceutical commercials for drugs with long lists of dangerous side effects. Notice how that is done when you watch the next drug commercial, and call out the name of the god at work—Hermes.

Our species is behaving like a cancer on the planet, operating out of relationship to all other life forms. We must realize how unique we are. All organisms manipulate their environment to some extent, but we are the only species that can consciously delineate the laws of nature and bend them to our advantage. Jung emphasized the absolute necessity of becoming more conscious, generally understood as becoming more conscious of the unconscious. Yet now we must also acknowledge our unique powers and the necessity of *consciously altering* our relationship with nature to become part of the web of existence. To do this we need to feel a deep emotional, spiritual, and symbolic relationship with the land as exhibited by indigenous cultures.

It is natural for a species to try to increase its dominance of a domain and for individuals within a given species to do the same; exemplary exceptions to this are the social insects: bees, wasps, termites, and ants, who are, by biomass, the most successful multicellular life forms on terrestrial earth. Humans express dominance through sexism, colonialism, racism, and through class and economic structures and other forms of hierarchical systems. Addressing climate change and the continued destruction of the rain forests are but two dramatic examples where a new paradigm of cooperation with all members of our species *across* national boundaries will be essential if we are to avoid truly apocalyptic conditions for ourselves and the extant species on our beautiful planet.

Increased consciousness will lead us to the uncomfortable awareness of the collective shadow each of us carries, that each of us is capable of inflicting unconscionable brutality upon our fellow human beings—torture, wars, and blindness to the suffering of the poor, the starving, and the refugees. We are all related, for better and for worse. Jung said the archetypal core of our shadow is Evil, a painful reality to face in ourselves and in what we see in the news of our world. It is an *opus contra naturum*, a work against nature, to overcome our *natural inclination* not to face the dark sides of our individual and collective shadows.

A more difficult work against nature, in a way, is to become conscious of the devastating effects our comfortable lives have upon the environment.

The Great Mother archetype, in her protective and nourishing form, wants all her children to have an abundance of food, safe drinking water, protection from the elements, and freedom from disease. The scientific and technological genius associated with the Greek god Apollo, and the structure and stability of order in economic systems that we can attribute to Saturn cooperate to satisfy the Great Mother. However, it would take four or five planet Earths to enable every human to live like an American. Now we must consciously and deliberately lessen our carbon and environmental footprints to be able to survive and live sustainably.

A Jungian Ecological Model for a Younger Generation

The spiritual dimension is the deepest, most significant aspect of our relationship with each other and with nature, and Jungian psychology excels in its ability to develop that domain. Unlike Freud, Jung maintained that spirituality was one of the highest forms of meaning and wholeness a human could experience. Jung focused on the greater importance of spirituality in the second half of life as one approaches death and questions about the meaning and significance of one's life intensifies. Native Americans offer another model that turns this approach on its head and presents an opportunity to make Jungian psychology more understandable and attractive to younger people who are becoming increasingly worried about their future on a planet that is deteriorating at an alarming rate. A 2021 survey on the effects of climate change on 10,000 youth ages 16–25 across ten countries found that 75% were frightened about their future, and 58% felt their governments had betrayed them and were not doing enough to avoid a climate catastrophe (University of Bath, September 14, 2021).

Many indigenous cultures have an initiation ceremony for boys when they hit puberty to help channel testosterone energy for the well-being of the tribe and inculcate the young male with an awesome spiritual sense beyond the sex drive. An adolescent Lakota Sioux boy went on a vision quest where he was put "on the hill" within a sacred space for four days without food and water. Family, friends, and the Holy Man prayed for him, and he prayed for himself, for a vision for his life, and for the appearance of a spirit animal, plant, landscape, or weather phenomena. These were unique images of the boy's essence—a *Black* Elk, a *Sitting* Bull (Buffalo), a *Red*

Cloud, etc. This was his "medicine," life guide, and teacher—a sense of his core being, the foundation, and the touchstone of his existence. A quest is like a near-death experience in that it puts maximum stress on the psyche that facilitates but doesn't guarantee a sense of one's essence.

Fred Gustafson, a dear friend, a Jungian analyst, Lutheran minister, and sun dancer, did several vision quests and wrote about his experiences in *Dancing Between Two Worlds* (Gustafson, 1997). According to him, you feel like you are going to die at the end of a four-day vision quest. I did a two-day vision quest on the Rosebud Reservation in South Dakota, and when I lay down after two days and closed my eyes, my head was filled with vivid, abstract images. It is humbling to be in nature virtually naked, with minimal shelter, and without food and water. One experiences nature in its many dimensions and feels how small we humans are in this vast and beautiful universe. Synchronistic events become more frequent as one sinks deeply into the archetypal domain. The vision quest is a solitary experience through which one comes to deeply appreciate one's connections to other humans and all creatures great and small.

I did not receive a spirit animal on my vision quest, but when doing a prayer round during the quest, for a fleeting moment, I had the overwhelming sense that my left leg was that of a spirit animal that had come to me in a dream some years earlier while I was training in Zurich. Two spirit animals appeared to me in dreams in Zurich, and one came to me in a shamanism workshop I did some years later after returning to the States. The most significant experience of the sacred in nature came in one of many big dreams I had in my last year of training. It was a single-image dream of a typical Wisconsin meadow with a hayfield in the foreground and insects flying above it. The typography was gently rolling with some trees on the horizon. It was a beautiful summer day with puffy white clouds in a blue sky. It was the most beautiful landscape I have ever seen; every atom in the dream glowed with a sacred inner light.

Spirit animals and sacred landscapes are like images of God in natural forms. The challenge is to embody that essence in how one lives one's life and to use the sacred experience as a touchstone for critical decisions, such as partner and career choices. Animals don't live in a vacuum; to fully appreciate your spirit animal, you must read about it, immerse yourself in its natural environment, and study its ways. Native Americans wear elements of the animal and dance its gait and make its sounds at pow wows and sacred gatherings, having carefully observed the animal on its home turf.

The Spirit in Land in the Upper Midwest

My meadow dream was a decisive factor in determining what state our young family would move to when I finished training. It was the inspiration for the Spirit in the Land weeklong seminars my wife and I conducted in 1991 and 1992: didactic and experiential events to integrate science, Native American spirituality, and Jungian psychology presented mostly by people deeply connected to the Wisconsin environment (www.jungianecopsychology.com/2022/02/spirit-in-land-interdisciplinary.html). The talks I gave were the genesis for writing *The Dairy Farmer's Guide to the Universe.* I have come to appreciate a powerful spirit in the land and seasons of the Upper Midwest that I was unaware of when I grew up in Wisconsin, before I left for graduate school in Berkeley in 1967. I have come to know that spirit by using scientific knowledge, mythology, symbols, dreams, Native American spirituality, imaginal psychology, and the *I Ching*, which uses agricultural and seasonal analogies to convey the wisdom of the Chinese sages. I conveyed these ideas in *Land, Weather, Seasons, Insects—An Archetypal View* (Merritt, 2013).

Scientific knowledge about the environment, Apollo's domain, is important in the Midwest, a region that perhaps lacks the visual splendor of some places in the world. As J. Baird Callicott describes it:

> The land aesthetic is sophisticated and cognitive, not naïve and hedonic; it delineates a refined taste in natural environments and a cultivated natural sensibility. The basis of such refinement or cultivation is natural history, and more especially, evolutionary and ecological biology . . . The beauty of a bog is a function of the palpable organization and closure of the interconnected living components. . . . Thus . . . an autonomous natural aesthetic must free itself from the prevailing visual bias.
>
> (Callicott, 1994, pp. 178, 181)

Phil Lewis, engaged by then Governor Gaylord Nelson to assess the natural resources of Wisconsin, described 72 "landscape personalities" in the state—Illinois has six (Carpenter, 2007). Each personality is like an eco-Self, a little cosmos—the beauty of the display of things and the proper arrangement and order that emerges from their interactions (Hillman, 1989, p. 21). The land aesthetic offers an experiential template for seeing our individual selves not as isolated beings, but as aspects of a cosmos.

I continue to embody the meadow dream when I exercise at Atwater Park in Milwaukee County, Wisconsin, beside Lake Michigan, one of the most magnificent bodies of fresh water in the world. The hillside is covered with native plants and wildflowers, and the lake generates its own ever-changing weather and environment—the lake effect. I remind myself when I go there almost daily, "This is what my soul looks like." I look at every element in the environment as an aspect of the gestalt of my soul. It is ever changing within different time frames: by the moment with a shift of wind off the lake or a cloud passing overhead, by the weather pattern, by the season, by the phenology of wildflower emergence, etc. The sounds change with the waves or the presence or absence of red-winged blackbirds and sea-gulls. Spring and fall bring bird migrations as they follow the shoreline. Midwestern air is full of the scents of life from the abundance and variety of plants, our green friends. One's soul emerges simultaneously with the *anima mundi*, the soul of the world, by loving attention paid to the particulars of the elements in the environment and noting their relationships (Hillman, 1992, pp. 101–130).

I often remind myself that the lake beds for the Great Lakes were carved out during the last glacial period that ended over 10,000 years ago and were initially filled with glacial melt. Vast glacial history time frames, past and future, press forward into consciousness. Six major Ice Ages engulfed the planet going back 3 billion of our planet's 4.5 billion years of existence. Multicellular life exploded during the Cambrian period following an Ice Age a billion years ago. Agriculture slowly emerged after the last glacial period, and it helped boost our numbers and eventually led to the rise of modern civilizations. Our species, gods of the Anthropocene Era, can now disrupt these billion-year cycles: Such is our power.

I think of these things in their many dimensions and time frames, not only as the dimensions of my soul but also as an analogy to Jung's description of the layers of the collective unconscious as a living museum with all levels in continual interaction with each other (Jung, 1961, pp. 158–162; Hannah, 1976, pp. 16–18). This nudges me beyond a conscious focus on the "I" and into Hillman's beehive model for consciousness—a holistic gestalt in which everything interacts and is interconnected.

Maintaining our psychic integrity and healthy boundaries is not unlike the challenge of protecting the Great Lakes that are incredibly fragile despite their size. The St. Lawrence seaway opened the Great Lakes to oceangoing ships that dump contaminated bilge water from other bodies of water, introducing invasive species like the alewives that exploded into the millions and whose rotting bodies stunk up the shorelines, like the zebra mussels, and the quagga mussels that now cover the lake bottoms and eliminate many of the native organisms that had formed the base of the Great Lakes food chain. The watershed for the lakes is only about twice the size of the surface area of the lakes themselves. It would take about 100 years to turn over the volume of water in some parts of the lakes. If the nearly 70-year-old pipeline crossing Mackinaw Straits between Lakes Michigan and Huron were to break, the toxic tar sands oil piped through from Alberta, Canada would contaminate the waters for decades to come.

An Homage to Native Wildflower Gardens

Gardening is a common and significant way to experience connections to the plant and animal worlds. I have a garden, but one that requires no work after the initial plantings. I have been pleasantly surprised, again and again, living in the city of Milwaukee by how much I enjoy the native wildflower gardens I planted in my front and back yards. No watering, no weeding, no lawn to cut—how could people not love that? Neighbors fertilize and apply herbicides and pesticides, then put up signs warning pets and children to stay off the turf for a couple days—what's wrong with that picture? I leave the dead plants over winter to watch the slow process of decay of the previous summer's growth, and I collect the autumn leaves from the street in front of my house and neighbors' houses to fertilize and mulch the soil. Leaf litter protects insects and critters that overwinter on the ground, like fireflies, giving them the opportunity to display their muted twinkling of phosphor-chemical lightning over the garden on warm summer evenings. Spring, Growth, Harvest, and Trial, the four phases in any cycle of change (Supreme, Success, Furthering, and Perseverance in Wilhelm's *I Ching*), can be experienced in the middle of a city with the phenology of flowering plants, their insect friends, and the birds that feast on the insects.

I was sitting on my front porch some summers ago, being nourished by the beauty of the plants, then appreciating the mixed assemblage of insects, when the next level of awareness hit me: I was witnessing the result of millions of years of co-evolution of pollinating insects with the flowering plants; a living symbiosis in my front yard. The eight-foot-tall wall of cup flowers forming the southern border with my neighbor's yard attracts bumblebees whose populations are in decline, as are so many insect species.

I planted over 100 milkweeds, the only plant on which the lovely monarch butterfly can reproduce. The monarch—emblem of the Entomological Society of America—is in precipitous decline due to replacement of milkweed habitat by farm crops, herbicide use, and systemic pesticides that poison the very nectar the insects suck from the flowers.

I spent hours in the wildflower garden with my 4-year-old grandson when he visited from Hong Kong. We collected insects, pill bugs, spiders, snails, and slugs (the latter two being all he can find in mid-city Hong Kong, much to his mother's chagrin). The terrarium on the front porch was better than any TV or video game for him. Kids have a natural fascination and bonding with nature, and research has proven how important a nature connection is for a child's development and sense of well-being (Scott et al., 2016, pp. 285–292).

These are examples of how we can meet Jung's challenge of uniting our cultured side with what he called the "two-million-year-old man within," what Fred Gustafson called the "Indigenous One within" (Jung, 1977, pp. 359–364, 396–397; Gustafson 1997, pp. 77–79). These are Jungian responses to Carl Sagan's challenge, as co-chair of Religion and Science for the Environment in 1992, that stressed the need to establish a sense of the sacred in the environment if we were to save it from the ravages of technology and corporate power (Sagan, 1992).

The Sacred in Jung's Alchemical Model for Therapy, Analysis, and the Environment

Re-establishing a sense of the sacred in nature was a goal in alchemy, Jung's main symbolic system. Alchemy, which flourished in secret from early Christianity until the rise of science in the seventeenth century, dealt with a projection of a post-Christian unconscious into the alchemist's vessels and retorts. They worked with the shadow side of Christianity, what the Christian focus on brightness, ethereal, and a spiritual *other*-worldliness had ignored and denigrated—the sexual, sensual, earthy feminine, and nature. Alchemists wrestled with these issues in imaginal and visionary ways while exploring the physical and chemical changes of the materials in their containers. This provided an imaginal framework for engaging the leadenness in their lives and transmuting it, at the personal and collective levels, into gold—that of highest value. The lead-to-gold metaphor was one of innumerable ways of symbolically describing the psychological and spiritual transformations they experienced. Many felt that Christ had saved the microcosm, the human soul, and they were working to re-sacralize the natural environment, a sense that got lost for most Christians in the evolution of Christianity. In 1939, Jung had a vision of Christ on the cross with a body of greenish gold, an alchemical Christ as he saw it. He interpreted the green-gold to represent the living quality, the life spirit that animates the cosmos; a sacred spirit in everything, living and material (Jung, 1961, pp. 210–211).

The alchemist's gold and Jung's description of the phenomenology of the Self are about the experience of something of ultimate importance and eternal truth. Anyone who gets close to such sacred power will have the following of a Moses, Jesus, Mohammed, or Buddha (CW14, par. 781–789). With Jung's descriptores of the phenomenology of the Self, we can appreciate multiculturalism at its most fundamental level—multiple valid spiritual traditions—a *spiritual ecology*. I can say "I have the best dog in the world," and you can say the same—and we are both right! From my cultural and historical origins, this is what feels like the eternal truth and of utmost value, comparable at a personal level to the experience of the Self as a spirit animal.

Jung argued that a sense of the numinous, the sacred, was essential in an individual and in a culture if they were to be whole (CW11, par. 735). This would include the educational system. Jung railed about the strictures of science, materialism, and rationalism—all important aspects of but one god in the Greek pantheon—Apollo. But domination by any one god becomes a cancer to a society. Scientists like Carl Sagan are in awe, as they should be, of the generative powers of the universe; a generativity that produced our species—we did not invent ourselves (Sagan, 1992). This a scientific sense of the sacred in nature that compliments an indigenous sense that can be realized by establishing a relationship with the "indigenous one within" our collective unconscious.

Jung strongly believed a paradigm shift was necessary to move individuals, cultures, and systems towards a vital wholeness. Attributes of the New Age paradigm, as Jung saw it, were a special role for the feminine, the emergence of new spiritual forms, Christian integration of vital elements of the "heathenism" they had been persecuting, and an end to the degradation of the environment (CW11, par. 745–746; Jung, 1961, pp. 339–340; Von Franz, 1975, pp. 36–37, 136, 145, 164–165). The symbol of a New Age/ Age of Aquarius paradigm shift is the most significant Jungian concept and framework for the dimensions of changes our species has to make in order to survive with some integrity and to live sustainably.

Archetypal Guidance from the *I Ching* for the New Age

The *I Ching*, a profound Chinese book of wisdom that greatly influenced Jung, offers an archetypal goal for negotiating the necessary changes that must occur in the paradigm shift. The message in Hexagram 42 is "Increase." An archetypal image, as are all hexagrams (combinations of six solid (yang) and/or broken (yin) lines), is that those with power, in whatever form, come down to help the less fortunate. The Wilhelm/Baynes translation declares

> This concept expresses the fundamental idea on which the Book of Changes is based. To rule truly is to serve. . . . A sacrifice of the higher element that produces an increase of the lower is called an out-and-out increase: *it indicates the spirit that alone has power to help the world* (emphasis added).
>
> (Wilhelm, 1967, p. 162)

To rule by serving in our society means addressing income inequality, sexism, and political, social, and health care inequalities. The inequality of the Anthropocene Era, our species' relationship to other living forms on the planet, calls for a change in economic systems to put the environment at the center instead of being a resource base and waste dump—a central premise for the green or sustainable economists. They call for wealth redistribution on a planetary level and spreading the work hours around the planet. Decreasing work hours by half allows workers to spend valuable time with family, friends, hobbies, and community building activities. Population numbers must also be limited; our species has exceeded the carrying capacity of planet Earth (Dietz and O'Neill, 2013).

A Paradigm Shift in the Therapist's Office

I illustrate how I work in analysis with the ecological dimensions of Jung's New Age paradigm shift by my work with young people. In the past several years, I've had more people in their 40s and younger enter my practice who are recovering from their evangelical and fundamentalist Christian upbringing and/or are anxious about the ecological state of the planet. The educational phase Jung saw in the analytic process plays an important role in working with these clients. Many indigenous cultures consider disease and loss of soul arising from loss of connection—to others and to the earth. Most analysands need a degree of education about how archetypes as historical dominants—Western cultural, economic, and spiritual—have left them without connections to their deeper selves, to others, and to the land (Merritt, 2012, pp. 54–87, 131–136). Analysts now have the significant role of educating their analysands about the archetypal underpinnings of our culture and guiding the analysands in establishing a connection to nature. In the course of the analytic work, I introduce concepts I have presented in this chapter. Particularly when working with recovering fundamentalists and evangelicals, I may well include my summary of Jung's analysis of Christianity that I have written about elsewhere (Merritt, 2012, pp. 54–70).

As analysts we are trained to work with dreams and symbols, things rarely discussed in university psychology programs and professional psychology training institutions. One's personal analysis is the most important ingredi-ent for a successful practice, and today many non-Jungian therapists do not have to undergo therapy to become therapists. Only by having a feeling for the symbolic in dreams and in the lives of the clients can an analyst relate to symbols in an authentic manner that is convincing to the analysand. It is usually up to the analyst to notice the symbols in the client's conscious and unconscious lives and hold the symbol for the analysand while guiding them in manifesting and embodying it in their lives. The Native American vision quest and spirit animal concept offers an excellent way to concep-tualize the work with numinous animals, plants, weather, and landscape phenomena in dreams.

It is especially important from an ecopsychological perspective for the analyst to notice dream symbolism that the analysand can use to connect them to the land in a deeper and maybe even a sacred manner, as illustrated by my Atwater Park and wildflower garden experiences that were inspired by my sacred meadow dream. Immersing oneself in the environment of the spirit animal or sacred landscape moves one towards an indigenous sense of the web of life and perhaps even an experience of the sacred intercon-nection of everything—the beauty of which the Greeks called the cosmos.

The analyst can help the more politically aware analysands view mod-ern culture from an archetypal, symbolic perspective, as illustrated in the idea of big corporations as narcissistic monsters now ruling the planet and destroying the environment. One can explore how polarization is amplified in American society when the God-on-our-side and good-versus-evil per-spectives of the evangelicals and fundamentalists are united with politics, short-circuiting the possibility of meaningful dialogue. The Greeks con-sidered Truth and Deception to be sisters, thwarting a gravitation towards absolutist positions. Charges of voter fraud are thinly disguised attempts to suppress the votes of minorities and the poor, violating Jesus' request to take in and feed the homeless and the hungry, and the archetypal message from Hexagram 42 for the powerful to help the less fortunate. These are but two of many expressions from different cultural traditions of the archetypal theme of redressing inequalities. The intra-psychic repression and suppres-sion of undesirable "little people within" that challenge the ego's power position is archetypically and thematically related at the political level to voter suppression and gerrymandering. This archetypal framing facilitates a linking of the personal to the cultural and the issues of our times, connec-tions that help reduce the indigenous sense of dis-ease.

I emphasize how ecology starts with our relationship with the "little peo-ple within" and how there is something in us, as part of nature and natural processes (ecological concepts, being an organism, and complexity theory mathematics), that produces dreams. Dreams emerge from a wholistic generative source that tries to move us to greater consciousness through compensatory images in dreams and our symptomology metaphorically expressed in dreams. Symbols are the transformative images in dreams that captivate our attention and, when properly worked with, transmute our dis-eased state in the process of moving us towards wholeness and greater con-sciousness. Symbols for Jungians always contain a mysterious unknown element that connects us in a deep-felt sense to the irrational, inexplicable, and eternal/archetypal, undermining a too literal, linear, and positivistic take on oneself and one's culture.

My best training for working in a symbolic and archetypal manner came from a strong emphasis on interpreting fairy tales. Legends and fairy tales are seen as compliments to the dominant spiritual and cultural tradi-tions, and the *Grimms'* and Russian fairy tales contained significant ele-ments of nature and the sensuous in their story lines. Walt Disney used the French Perrot version of Cinderella, but the *Grimms'* version is psy-chologically more powerful and earthy. It was not a fairy godmother who bestowed ballroom dresses upon Cinderella, but birds in a tree that grew from a twig planted in her mother's grave and watered by Cinderella's tears. Trees are universal Self symbols and bridge all three realms—roots (the unconscious), trunk (human conscious domain), and crown (sky and spirit). Birds aided Cinderella in sorting out the good from the bad lentils, metaphorically discerning what nourishes one's psyche and what is harmful to it; birds brought consciousness to the prince about the unseen damage being done to the feminine; and two birds pecked out the eyes of the stepsisters, destroying their deadly and envious narcissistic gaze. Especially when working with women living out the Cinderella archetypal pattern, one can connect the personal to the collective and illustrate where they are in the alchemical transformative process by noting what role they assume in the story.

Most of my practice has been with men, work that has illustrated the connection between the personal and the collective, and the link between their complexes and dream motifs to the archetypal pattern as expressed in the Grimms' fairy tale "Iron Hans" (popularized by Robert Bly in his 1990 book *Iron John*). The story is about a boy coming of age with the aid of a wild man and deals with critical issues for men of sex and aggression. Jung maintained that the animal soul, the animal ancestor level of the collective unconscious, is associated with instincts and animal drives, particularly sexuality (Jung, 1973, p. 427; CW10, par. 105). Robert Bly founded a men's movement based on the *Grimms'* fairy tale, and several of my analysands have participated in various aspects of that movement. I ran a small men's group centered around a discussion of the tale as it related to our lives, and we participated in group ceremonies that connected us to nature. It was a powerful healing experience for each of us, especially in the shared stories of the pain suffered in the relationships with our fathers.

It is the pathologies, the metaphoric lead in our lives, that provide the entrée to the inner realm when things fall apart (that's how the light gets in, as Leonard Cohen reminds us). By being able to face chaos and collapse while in the container of analysis, healing symbols can emerge that the analyst must recognize and then guide the analysand to use the symbol to establish a new foundation and touchstone in their psyche. The more purely ecological dimensions are clear when the symbols appear in the form of spirit animals, as mentioned before. To experience the bodily aspects of incarnating a symbol, I also encourage my analysands to practice yoga, tai chi, chi gung, meditation, etc., depending on their passions, expertise, and abilities. Once a new foundation is established, the analysand can rather naturally become involved in the worldly activities and activism. Thoreau spent only two years at Walden to establish his spiritual and philosophical base, after which he became involved in the abolitionist movement in the mid-1800s.

Jung said one cannot live without a sense of meaning that comes from seeing one's unique place in a bigger whole. The pursuit of meaning for the analysand becomes more important than consumption in a capitalistic sense. This is an ecological goal and antidote to consumerism, for we find meaning through our *relationship* with the little people within, with our society, and with the natural world out of which we evolved and to which we return after death.

The Magnitude of the Change Required

Before we talk about resiliency, remediation, and adaptation to environmental disasters like those arising from climate change, we must become fully conscious of the magnitude of the underlying issues and causes. This necessitates an understanding of our cultural, economic, spiritual, educational, and political evolution to this point of our dysfunctional relationship with nature as referenced earlier. To this end, every layer of the personal and collective unconscious can be analyzed, starting with the ego and family layers, then the collective unconscious layers of the national, cultural (West vs. East), and indigenous and animal ancestors (Merritt, 2017, pp. 54–55, 2019). The corporate model must be changed. We must address the polarizations in our society, a seemingly insurmountable task when a substantial proportion of the American electorate believe "alternative facts" and conspiracy theories. The effects of climate change are beginning to dwarf all other human problems. It's as if a metaphoric diagnosis of cancer was given over 30 years ago when climate expert James Hansen testified in Congress about the developing danger of climate change. Not nearly enough has been done since then to treat the disease. The cancer is now early stage 4, where metastasis is occurring with potential for catastrophic rapid change (environmental tipping points). We are at a point where drastic and major changes must be made quickly and at all levels in order to survive. It takes this level of awareness of the problems and a deep concern to move us into the magnitude and multidimensions of a paradigm shift—Jung's most important concept for our times.

In an interview for BBC TV in 1959, Jung stated emphatically, "We need more psychology . . . because the only real danger is man himself. . . . His psyche should be studied because we are the origin of all coming evil"

(Jung, 1977, p. 436). Robert Lewis Stevenson woke the literary, spiritual, and general public to that shocking awareness with the publication of his wildly popular *The Strange Case of Dr. Jekyll and Mr. Hyde* back in 1886. Change must begin with the individual in relation to the shadow. Activists are less likely to burn out when they realize "we have met the enemy and the enemy is us." The worldview and negative consequences of late-stage capitalism are part of us, and things will change as slowly as it takes to change our inner lives and come to terms with our complexes. I have written how Jungian concepts of the Shadow, illustrated by Mr. Hyde, the anima and animus, the Self, and Jungian ecopsychology could be incorporated into our educational system as one element for moving into the New Age paradigm shift (Merritt, 2012, pp. 117–124).

Every psychological system has made unique contributions to understanding our dysfunctional relationship with the environment and developing a broader application of ecological concepts (Winter, 1996, pp. 62–269; Merritt, 2017, pp. 51–54). The Jungian contributions to ecopsychology help us to understand environmental problems from an archetypal and symbolic perspective, how to work with that perspective with analysands, and provide a framework for moving forward within the broad dimensions of a paradigm shift. There is an abundance of activities and actions we can engage in to manifest the archetypal aspects of our sense of self and place, such as those listed on Carl Golden's Tree of Life website. (www.treeoflife counseling.life/essays/ecopsychology.html). These include nature-oriented awareness practices like mindfulness and contemplative practices; earth work like environmental activism, education, and bioregionalism; nature-based psychological practices like wilderness retreats, vision fasts, and walkabouts; ecotherapy like despair and empowerment work and using nature as a therapist; and ritual and art like earth-centered festivals and seasonal celebrations. I encourage my analysands to experience a Native American sweat lodge ceremony if they have the opportunity. This powerful ceremony, called an *inipi* by the Lakota Sioux, can give one a deep experience of indigenous, earth-based spirituality, what a psychiatrist friend has called "the ultimate spiritual technology."

A Wakening

The pandemic gave us and opportunity for our species to evolve into greater consciousness, forcing us to face existential issues about life and death and demonstrating how interconnected and interrelated we are on many levels. The lockdowns reminded us of the importance of human relationships for social animals like ourselves. It highlighted stark inequalities in American society wherein the poor, with more underlying health conditions, were more vulnerable while at the same time being recognized as "essential workers" in the food, transportation, sanitary industries, etc. Together with the absence of early central government coordination, a deteriorated public health system, and the politization around wearing masks and vaccinations, America led the world with deadly ineptness in response to the pandemic.

The fear, confusion, and massive upheavals caused by the virus have loosened up rigid social and economic systems, offering a rare opportunity for major changes. This could propel us to finally start on the path toward a gigantic, systemic overhaul that moves us towards the paradigm shift Jung predicted in 1940. We have a lot of work to do, and the clock is running out.

References

Bly, R. 1990. *Iron John: A Book About Men*. Reading, MA: Addison Wesley.

Callicott, J. 1994. "The land aesthetic". In K. C. Chapple and M. E. Tucker, Eds. *Ecological Prospects: Scientific, Religious, and Aesthetic Perspectives*. Albany, NY: State University of New York Press.

Carpenter, T. 2007. "Phil Lewis-workin' on the railroad: Regional design—creating frameworks for quality of life, peace & survival". *Fitchburg Voices*, August 18. https://fitchburgvoices.blogspot.com/2006/08/phil-lewis-workin-on-railroad.html

Dietz, R. and O'Neill, D. 2013. *Enough Is Enough: Building a Sustainable Economy in a World of Finite Resources*. San Francisco, CA: Berrett-Koehler Publishers, Inc.

Gustafson, F. 1997. *Dancing Between Two Worlds: Jung and the Native American Soul*. Mahwah, NJ: Paulist Press.

Hannah, B. 1976. *Jung: His Life and Work*. Boston, MA: Shambala.

Hillman, J. 1988. "Going bugs". *Spring*, 40: 40–72.

———. 1989. "Cosmology for the soul: From universe to cosmos". *Sphinx*, 2: 17–33.

———. 1992. *The Thought of the Heart and the Soul of the World*. Woodstock, CT: Spring Publications.

Jung, C. 1961. *Memories, Dreams, Reflections*. Aniela Jaffe, Ed. Richard and Claire Winston, Trans. New York: Random House.

———. 1968. "Alchemical studies (CW 13)". In Herbert Read, Michael Fordham, Gerhard Adler and William McGuire, Eds. R. F. C. Hull, Trans. *Collected Works of C. G. Jung*. Princeton, NJ: Princeton University Press.

———. 1969a. "The structure and dynamics of the psyche (CW 8)". In Herbert Read, Michael Fordham, Gerhard Adler and William McGuire, Eds. R. F. C.

Hull, Trans. *Collected Works of C. G. Jung*. Princeton: Princeton University Press.

———. 1969b. "Psychology and religion: West and east (CW 11)". In Herbert Read, Michael Fordham, Gerhard Adler and William McGuire, Eds. R. F. C. Hull, Trans. *Collected Works of C. G. Jung*. Princeton: Princeton University Press.

———. 1970a. "Civilization in transition (CW 10)". In Herbert Read, Michael Fordham, Gerhard Adler and William McGuire, Eds. R. F. C. Hull, Trans. *Collected Works of C. G. Jung*. Princeton: Princeton University Press.

———. 1970b. "Mysterium coniunctionis (CW 14)". In Herbert Read, Michael Fordham, Gerhard Adler and William McGuire, Eds. R. F. C. Hull, Trans. *Collected Works of C. G. Jung*. Princeton: Princeton University Press.

———. 1973. "Letters. Vol. 1: 1906–1950". In Gerhard Adler, Ed. R. F. C. Hull, Trans. Princeton, NJ: Princeton University Press.

———. 1977. *C. G. Jung Speaking: Interviews and Encounters*. William McGuire and R. F. C. Hull, Eds. Princeton, NJ: Princeton University Press.

———. 1997. *Interpretation of Visions*. Claire Douglass, Ed. Princeton, NJ: Princeton University Press (Previously published as *The Visions Seminars*, 1976. Zurich, Switzerland: Spring Publications).

Merritt, D. 2012. *The Dairy Farmer's Guide to the Universe: Jung Hermes and Ecopsychology. Volume 1: Jung and Ecopsychology*. 1st ed. Fisher King Press.

———. 2013. *Land, Weather, Seasons, Insects: An Archetypal View* (Vol. 4).

———. 2017. "Ecopsychology: Psyche and the environment". In A. Chone, I. Hajec and P. Hamman, Eds. *Rethinking Nature: Challenging Disciplinary Boundaries*. London and New York, NY: Routledge.

———. 2019. "Jungian ecopsychology for the younger generation, Carol Koziol, interviewer". *Canadian Ecopsychology Network Interview Series: Ecopsychology Voices*. https://jungchicago.org/blog/ecopsychology-voices-jungian-ecopsychology-for-the-younger-generation-with-dennis-merritt/

Sagan, C. 1992. "To avert a common danger". *Parade Magazine*, 10–12, March.

Schwartz, R. 1997. *Internal Family Systems*. New York, NY: Guilford Press.

Scott, B., Amel, E., Koger, S. and Manning, C. 2016. *Psychology for Sustainability*. 4th ed. New York, NY and London: Routledge.

University of Bath. 2021. *Government Inaction on Climate Change Linked to Psychological Distress in Young People—New Study*. Press Release, September 14. www.bath.ac.uk/announcements/government-inaction-on-climate-change-linked-to-psychological-distress-in-young-people-new-study/

Von Franz, M.-L. 1975. *C. G. Jung: His Myth in Our Time*. London: Hodder & Stoughton.

Wilhelm, R., Trans. 1967. *The I Ching or Book of Changes*. Cary Baynes, English Trans. Princeton, NJ: Princeton University Press.

Winter, D. 1996. *Ecological Psychology: Healing the Split Between Planet and Self*. New York, NY: Harper Collins College Publishers.

Chapter 8

The Jungian Analyst in Between Life and Death

Clinical Ethics in an Age of Pandemic

John R. White

Introduction

"Death and life are in the gift of the tongue, those who indulge it must eat the fruit it yields" (Proverbs 18:21 NJB). Death and life can indeed be "in the gift of the tongue," and those of us who are practitioners of so-called "talk therapy" are perhaps well advised to keep that fact in mind. Death in particular often lurks at least at a subterranean level in our therapy sessions, while at other times, it percolates to the surface, often in the form of death anxiety and in psychological defenses such as death denial. Death-related issues are, in fact, important factors in psychological health and illness and are also understandably exacerbated in an age of pandemic.

Over the last three years, practicing Jungian psychoanalysis amidst the current pandemic and related situations, I have often been struck by unusual resonances in my own psyche as I attempt to aid my patients to deal with death anxiety. At first, I assumed that those experiences arose simply because of the intensity of death anxiety in the current time—my patients', mine, and the collective's. As time went on, however, I doubted that that explanation was sufficient and began to recognize distinct but related phenomena seeming to accompany the death anxiety. As I will suggest, these experiences, which some of my colleagues also report, may pose not only a clinical but also a central ethical concern for psychoanalytic clinical practice. This ethical component can be articulated in terms of what the ancient philosophers sometimes called the "death of the soul," an image which, though not found in psychoanalytic literature,[1] relates to the main concern of this chapter, death anxiety.

In the following, I will discuss three interconnected themes. First, I will look at death and death anxiety as clinical phenomena, something I will undertake with the help of both Carl Jung and especially Robert Langs.

DOI: 10.4324/9781003252993-9

Second, I will derive some ethical ideas from ancient Greek and Roman philosophy, relevant both to the symptoms of death anxiety and to the ancient notion of "death of the soul." Finally, I will draw some implications from these ideas, regarding the development of a clinical ethics.

Two Conceptions of Death

Carl Jung and Robert Langs offer quite different conceptions of death. Though this contrast amounts to something like an opposition, as we will see, understanding the nature of the difference will both help us to interpret the ancient philosophers as well as see how these two conceptions can in fact be understood as supplementing each other, at least in certain respects.

Jung's notion of death is bound up with his conception of the teleology of the psyche (Jung, 1931, 1934). Like many ancient and medieval philosophers, Jung considered the soul or psyche to have in internal, inherent impulse toward its own development, described in terms of both an end or purpose (*telos*) and the process driving toward that purpose (teleology). Jung writes, "Life is teleology *par excellence*; it is the intrinsic striving towards a goal, and the living organism is a system of directed aims which seek to fulfill themselves. The end of every process is its goal" (Jung, 1934).

Following this assumption, therefore, Jung considers death something more than the mere cessation of life. Rather, death is the end of a process, the life process itself, which must, in some way, Jung thinks, actually be the goal or *telos* of life. Indeed, Jung noted that he had been a witness to a number of dream series of patients who were or who, at some point in their treatment, had begun the process of dying. In each case, Jung maintains, the unconscious prepares for death and appears surprisingly untroubled by it, which further suggested to him that death is an internal element of the life process, not something extrinsic to it (Jung, 1934).

In contrast to Jung, Freudian Robert Langs treats death fundamentally as the cessation of physical life. In his later work, following Ernest Becker and the latter's well-known book on death anxiety (Becker, 2020), Langs came to consider death, death-related traumas, and death anxiety to be the central sources of psychological conflict, rather than sexuality, the traditional Freudian view (Langs, 2004b, 2004a, 2005). For virtually the final twenty years of his life, Langs sought to understand the psychological meaning of each of these death-related phenomena and how they impacted psychological life. Based on his study of evolutionary biology, Langs came to the unhappy conclusion that human beings are in fact failures of evolution (Langs, 2004b, 2010). The reason he thought so is that he believed survival favors those who are in denial of death and death anxiety. Consequently, those who are more likely to survive are also those who are least psychologically healthy and those most likely to do damage to the survival of our species (Langs, 2010).[2]

We can see in these two conceptions of death a stark contrast: For Langs, death is the cessation of life, a universal phenomenon dominating everyone's psychic life. Consistent with this view, Langs believed that all talk of an afterlife as, for example, many popular religions do, is a straightforward case of death denial, provoked by death anxiety (Langs, 2004b, 2010). In contrast, for Jung, these same religions offer something positive to people by treating death as something more than the cessation of life, as a process in which death is, in some sense, the *fulfillment* of life. In this respect, Jung was closer to traditional philosophy and religion than Langs. Plato, for example, calls philosophy a "meditation on death," because learning how to live is also learning how best to die. The only answer to death on this classical philosophical model is to answer a decisively qualitative question: "How well did I live?" But this conception also assumes that human life is about something beyond the issue of survival and therefore also beyond the range of evolutionary biology, something likely to be doubted in an age in which materialism and consumerism appear to dominate much of the psychological landscape (White, 2022).

Langs on the Forms and Symptoms of Death Anxiety

Though Langs wrote literally hundreds of pages on death-related issues, his contributions tend to be little known. I will, therefore, hazard a brief summation of some of his conclusions since they seem particularly illuminating in a time of pandemic. Langs differentiated three kinds of death anxiety: existential, predatory, and predator death anxieties. Each form of death anxiety has somewhat different indications and symptoms, yet, according to Langs, they nonetheless share one thing in common: Their basic defense is denial (Langs, 2004a, 2004b). Let me sketch each briefly.

The most universal and possibly the most important form, for Langs, is existential death anxiety: anxiety over death, annihilation, and ultimate demise. Langs believes that this form of death anxiety is virtually always present in psychotherapy. Its primary indications include (1) unconsciously motivated avoidance of rules, boundaries, and impingements, rooted in avoidance of the ultimate boundary, death; (2) inclination to obliterate traumatic emotions and meanings, since traumas resonate with the anxiety over death. Denial is its primary defense, according to Langs, especially forms which can create the illusion that one, in some sense, "defeats death," such as perceptual blindness, obliteration of thoughts, and illusions or delusions of immortality.

There are also behavioral forms of such denial, which are especially interesting in our own time. These might include manic celebrations, irrational acts of violence, murder and other crimes, seeking excessive power and wealth, and substantive rule violations. In each of these we can see the unconscious dread of limits of any kind and the unconscious aspiration to make decisions which feel, on the surface, as if they annihilate the power of death, though in many cases such behaviors are in fact doing death's work. As one would expect, entrapment anxieties and an unconscious dread of a secured therapeutic frame are among the effects for therapy.

The second form is predatory death anxiety, the anxiety over being killed or victimized in some way. Unlike existential death anxiety with its defensive perceptual blindness, predatory death anxiety typically includes a higher perceptiveness, because there is, of course, a need to assess actual dangers. According to Langs, its primary defense is a combination: on the one hand, a fight-flight-freeze reaction, just as one would expect from the fear of victimization, but also, on the other hand, some tendency toward denial. The combination arises because it is often and even typically caregivers who are the perpetrators. Consequently, the victim is put in the difficult situation of both fearing and protecting the caregiver. For such a person, Langs maintains, changes in the ground rules of therapy—the rules that produce a secured therapeutic frame—produce anxiety that one will be a victim, since violations of or alterations in boundaries are essential to the original victimization by a caregiver.

The third form is predator death anxiety, that is, the anxiety that, having (literally or figuratively) killed someone or something, one will suffer unbearable consequences. The indication for this includes self-punitive, self-defeating behavior, and unbearable guilt and self-image. Its primary defense is denial, precisely because of unbearable guilt and self-image. The effects for therapy, for both therapist and patient, include fear of activating painful forms of guilt, self-recrimination, and self-punitive behaviors. For therapists, Langs notes, deep unconscious guilt is a primary issue, in part because many aspects of today's accepted forms of psychotherapy are unconsciously predatory toward patients, especially due to their failure to recognize the importance of the secured therapeutic frame.

Frequently, a person has more than one of these forms of death anxiety, according to Langs, and in each case, issues associated with what is traditionally called the therapeutic or analytic frame are essential (Langs, 2004a). This is because the frame is a set of conditions which act as boundaries, and boundaries resonate unconsciously with the ultimate boundary, which is death. Additionally, Langs believes that embedded in deeper levels of the unconscious is a kind of *wisdom system*, collecting, as it were, the wisdom of the species, and also possessing an ethical system of its own, best described in terms of the talion law, "An eye for an eye, a tooth for a tooth."

Failure to appreciate the various forms of death anxiety, Langs contends, poses a grave challenge for psychoanalytic styles of therapy (Langs, 2004a, 2004b). Death anxiety, being, for Langs, the deepest source of psychic conflict, cannot be adequately treated without sufficient feelings of security on the part of the patient. However, a secured therapeutic environment also produces a clinical paradox: On the one hand, it is positive because it gives the patient the sense of being secure, held, and contained; on the other hand, it also produces the negative situation of bringing death anxiety to the surface, since the frame, with its relatively rigid boundaries, resonates with death, the ultimate boundary. Hence, it is only within secured frame therapy that one can safely treat death anxiety, and yet secured frame therapy also produces or at least amplifies death anxiety in each of its forms, thus tending to provoke psychological defenses, especially denial. Furthermore, this denial is itself a potent issue in therapy because it is just this defense, Langs maintains, which blocks access to the deeper unconscious wisdom and ethical systems mentioned earlier.

We should, of course, not be surprised to see death anxiety not only emerging but, in fact, running amok in our society during a pandemic, given the life-and-death issues the latter implies. Certainly, the pandemic is the most obvious socially wide cause of death anxiety, but it is equally clear through reactions to, for example, the recent US presidential election (2020) as well as the recent protests (such as Black Lives Matter) that there are multiple ways in which death anxiety is being enacted socially and which most of us who are mental health professionals are also seeing in our clinical work.

As one would expect, with the pandemic, existential death anxiety is most pronounced. Langs mentions among the indications of existential death anxiety, as we already saw, resistance to any impingements and boundaries, perceptual blindness, illusions and delusions of immortality, and manic celebrations. Consider the many extreme reactions to wearing masks or social distancing, as if they were onerous impingements; or undercutting medical experts without having medical authority oneself, a classic case of defensive perceptual blindness; or illusions and delusions of immortality and manic celebrations, ranging from simply ignoring the strictures around caring for oneself and others during a pandemic all the way to "COVID parties" at many universities and other explicit rejections of reasonable rules or policies, including by people at the highest levels of government. These are only illustrations, and they could be multiplied exponentially, but perhaps most interesting is that there are not only high-profile cases but many, such as COVID parties, that, for at least a time, became more or less routine, demonstrating the extent to which existential death anxiety is all too alive and well.

Though existential death anxiety understandably dominates the scene, both predatory and predator death anxiety are also pronounced during the current crises. Consider the many examples of conflicts of trust toward the government and toward medical authorities, where one, at times, assumes the policies being put forth should be trusted (especially when coming from one's favored political party), yet at other times not, sometimes invoking one's purported Constitutional rights against them—the combination of hypervigilance and denial being a hallmark of predatory death anxiety. Also, predator death anxiety is quite widespread, for example in unnecessarily taking other people's lives into one's hands and simultaneously experiencing extreme unconscious guilt, self-recrimination, and self-punishment by exposing oneself to the very same dangers. Predator death anxiety may also be expressed in growing consciousness of White privilege due to Black Lives Matter, as in the patient of mine who became ambivalent about life projects clearly advantageous to herself and in no way disadvantageous to others, on the grounds that others did not have the same opportunities. Such unconscious self-defeating attitudes and actions on the part of those becoming aware of their privilege, though understandable, rarely help the social causes which provoke them.

It seems to me that, given the current pandemic and other stressors, there is more than enough evidence of the basic truth of what Langs sees, and that anxiety over physical death, the cessation of life, is not only widespread currently in our society but that the indications and symptoms of death anxiety are wreaking havoc in a number of different ways. The fact of the matter is that anxiety over death is not only a common and an intense source of psychic distress but that it requires an analytic approach which can reach the relatively deep sectors of the human mind.

However, there is another level to this issue with which I suggest Langs' approach cannot adequately deal. Langs' assumptions about the psyche, as outlined earlier, differ from Jung's in certain respects, and if one assumes—as I do—that Jung is closer to the truth on this issue, there must always be a certain dissatisfaction with Langs' treatment. Two central premises which Jung assumes and Langs does not are (1) that the psyche has a teleology, that is, that it is purposeful and that that purpose, in part, expresses itself in death; that, in other words, physical death is not only something to be avoided, but that physical death, beyond being the cessation of life, also retains a meaning because it is, in some sense, the *telos* or goal of the life process. Jung also assumes (2) what he calls the "Self," a divine-like principle in the psyche, drawing the individual ego and its psychic life toward itself, essentially playing the same role that the ancient and medieval philosophers attributed to the divine as a final cause. Langs had no place for such a principle, and, as we might imagine, death must look quite different if one thinks there is a divine principle actively drawing the psyche, even potentially into death, or not.

Life and Death of the Soul

Now Jung was aware that his idea of the soul's teleology was, in fact, an ancient philosophical teaching and that the nineteenth-century discovery of the soul or psyche on which he based his work was, in fact, a rediscovery, reaching back to the ancient philosophers. He was also aware that this concept of the Self or of a divine-like image in the psyche which draws the ego toward itself for the sake of greater realization of the psyche's potential was a reiteration of an ancient teaching, as when he calls the Self the "center and circumference" of the psyche—an image of the divine drawn directly from the fourth-century philosopher and theologian St. Augustine.

If we follow the trail back to those same ancient philosophical sources, we notice that, interestingly enough, the dominant ancient philosophical traditions—those of the Platonic and of the Aristotelian variety, for example—typically held both to the idea of a teleologically oriented psyche, often including the idea that death is a meaningful final act to life, *and* a recognition of some of the indications and symptoms Langs describes around death anxiety, especially existential death anxiety. Consequently, they offer a psychologically interesting analysis of those experiences around death and death anxiety, one which also includes a pronounced ethical component and assumes some awareness of the divine as an ordering principle of the soul. The basic source of experience of the divine was attained through the exercise of something the philosophers termed "*nous*," often infelicitously translated as "reason," because *nous* refers not so much to thinking or logic, as we often think of "reason" nowadays, as to the human capacity to be responsive to the divine and to order one's life according to that experience of the divine, to what that experience reveals about the order of the cosmos, and what it reveals about one's place within the cosmos (Voegelin, 1995, 2000).

Following philosopher Eric Voegelin and speaking in broad and schematic terms—since the ancient philosophers were not in any sense monolithic—we can say what we might call the broadly Platonic-Aristotelian experiences of the psyche were articulated by the philosophers in terms of a set of tensions (White, 2019). The first is imaged as a kind "vertical" tension. On the one hand, there is what we might call the "upward pull" of the *nous*, the capacity of the human being to be responsive to what is divine and immortal, an aspect of the human being which nineteenth-century philosophers sometimes referred to as "spirit" rather than "soul." On the other hand, there is the body and the instinctual drives associated with it which, if not properly cultivated, tend to pull the psyche "downward," as it were, toward a purely instinctual existence, that is, toward the *apeiron* or "nothingness," the world of the purely mortal. Thus, the soul or psyche exists "in between" the upward pull of immortalizing *nous* and downward pull of uncultivated, mortalizing instincts or passions. Plato coins the word *metaxis* to describe this experience, which can be translated as the "In-Between" (Voegelin, 1995). A generally healthy soul, on this model, is both responsive to the noetic pull from above—"noetic" being the adjectival form of *nous*—and mediates the latter's influence by ordering the body and the instincts, which is symbolized as "below," in terms of that higher pull. Only on condition that the entire human being is ordered according to that pull from above can one live in harmony with one's genuine nature, according to this model, since all human powers are thereby governed by the same higher principle. In contrast, if one does not seek a life responsive to the pull of the *nous*, ordering soul and body in its light, some level of disharmony is inevitable, as well as a tendency toward the "nothingness" of mortality, that is, toward existence exclusively within the realm of "mortalizing passion," what was sometimes termed the "death of the soul" (Voegelin, 1995, 2000).

Now it is worth noticing that the *nous*, the capacity and receptivity of the soul to divine influence and ordering, functions in a way substantially similar, though not identical, to Jung's notion of the "Self." I suggested earlier that "reason" is a less-than-adequate translation of the *nous* because the former tends to be associated with thinking and reasoning, whereas the *nous* is a receptive and responsive principle of *understanding*, which attains to a purportedly divine order and also directs a cultivation of the soul and body by means of its understanding. Similarly, as Ellenberger points out, the English translation of Jung's *das Selbst* as "the Self" has too subjective an overtone: It might be more literally translated as "the Itself," suggesting a fully objective principle imaged in the psyche but which, in some way, stands in itself—among other things as a working ideal of wholeness. Thus, there are similarities between the *nous* of the ancient philosophers and the Self of Jung, and the similar images used to discuss them pointed out earlier, such as the drawing of the psyche toward itself, therefore make some sense. Further, the diverse orientations of noetic pulling from above and the gravitational pull downward of the uncultivated instincts and passions is perhaps rendered somewhat more existential in the philosophers than it is in Jung, but in practice, Jung's articulation of the "transcendent function" (Jung, 1969), as something which mediates—that is, is In-Between—conscious and unconscious, balancing the opposites, is, I take it, an attempt to articulate the same point. For our purposes, therefore, I will assume some level of equivalence between the ancient symbol of the *nous* and Jung's symbol of the Self, even if they are not wholly identical.[3]

According to the ancient teaching, any attempt to use the *nous*, the understanding of and receptive participation in the divine, for purposes other than both relating to the divine and ordering the soul and body accordingly, invariably derails it and brings with it some psychopathological disturbances (Voegelin, 1995). That is to say, any use of the capacity for participation in the divine, for example, to foster disorder, to ignore the divine order, or, for example, to deny the divine order by positing dissociated or idealizing ideologies, or any of several other possible misuses, will, by necessity, throw the teleology of the psyche off course, leading it to pathologies of various kinds. Not only is the body such that it can be well or ill and is invariably subject to death, the soul can also be well or ill and, indirectly, subject to death. The soul becomes subject to death not by actual death, but rather by subjecting itself to mortalizing passion, rather than by cultivating and ordering itself and the instincts and passions through participation in the immortal and divine, via the *nous*.

Thus, a one-sided, disordered relationship to the tension of existence means domination by mortalizing passion or, in other words, the *death of the soul*, as one lives by what the philosophical tradition often called *vice*, the opposite of virtue, a life, in some ways, worse than physical death. The death of the soul is, in fact, a "living death" because the soul is not annihilated through psychological disorder, but lives; yet it lives in opposition to itself because it lives contrary to its natural orientation toward the divine or toward what Jung calls the Self. The soul, on this account, is "meant" to be ordered by the *nous* (or the Self), to live in the "In-Between" of life responsive to the Self, counteracting the downward pull of the body and the instinctual psyche by also cultivating the latter toward the Self. Failing to do so results in (1) disharmony and splitting of mortal and immortal aspects of human nature; (2) the predominance of indiscriminate impulses, instincts, and desires: "mortalizing passion" or vice. Such a life is a "being-toward-death" which, far from being a characteristic of existence per se, as Martin Heidegger suggests (Heidegger, 2010), the ancient philosophers would probably think is a characteristic only of the person living according to the death of the soul. In contrast, when one lives in the In-Between, living a fully human psychic and bodily life yet doing so under the influence of the divine principle, the entire being of the person, in principle, partakes in the immortalizing divine.

Cicero, the great Roman philosopher and statesman from the first century BCE, though substantially later than Plato and Aristotle, is nonetheless conversant enough in these traditions that he offers an analysis of the person who refuses to allow the *nous* to order the soul, in his *Tuscalan Disputations*. He writes:

> As there are diseases of the body, so there are diseases of the soul; the
> diseases are generally caused through a confusion of the mind by twisted

opinions, resulting in a state of corruption; the diseases of this type can arise only through a rejection of reason [in the sense of the *nous*, JRW].

(Cicero, 2018)

We notice here that Cicero speaks of "twisted opinions," suggesting a kind of cognitive derailment of the soul through the rejection or abuse of the *nous* or, in Jungian terms, through rejection of the pull and invitation of the Self. But this cognitive derailment, according to Cicero, does not remain in the order of thought, but results in *corruption*, again suggesting that refusing to be ordered by the divine principle is not a mere cognitive mistake, but has as its existential consequence that one's very nature becomes corrupted, in a psychological but also in a substantially ethical sense of the term. The assumption here, as with the earlier Platonic-Aristotelian picture, is that the soul is in tension between partaking of the immortalizing divine and the mortalizing downward pull of uncultivated passions, and how one relates to each of those pulls decides the extent to which one is psychologically and ethically corrupted.

Thus, according to Cicero, the rejection of *nous* leads to a number of consequences, including *anxietas*—evidently, the first attempt to delineate and analyze anxiety in Western history. Besides anxiety, other syndromes also arise from this rejection, among which Cicero lists: restless money-making, status-seeking, womanizing, overeating, addiction to delicacies and snacks, wine-tippling, irascibility, lust for fame, stubbornness, rigidity of attitude, misogyny, and misanthropy.

Obviously, this list sounds quite modern—like Cicero was standing in line at whatever was the ancient Roman equivalent of the grocery store, reading the tabloids. Furthermore, not only a good deal of contemporary psychological research but also pop psychological articles in magazines and online discuss these same issues widely. Given how widespread these issues are, in fact, we might be inclined to wonder how well we are doing in the mental health professions, but this is not simply an issue of our profession but more associated—if Cicero and the philosophers are on to something—with an entire society which attempts to alleviate its existential death anxieties in various forms of consumption rather than in facing them and the symptoms they produce.

However, a further point of interest is how many examples on this list are similar to those Langs described as being symptomatic of existential death anxiety. Cicero explicitly mentions anxiety itself, but also many of the symptoms he mentions represent either an inflationary "breaking of boundaries" (such as restless money-making and status-seeking), which, as Langs comments, are attempts to challenge death, or a movement toward unconscious oblivion (like stubbornness, overeating, womanizing, etc.), all ways of avoiding anxiety through death denial or through the diversions of "mortalizing passion." Furthermore, some of these symptoms fit into Langs' description of predator death anxiety because they suggest the will to domination (Augustine's *libido dominandi*), such as womanizing, misogyny, and misanthropy. In other words, it follows from the ancient analysis of these syndromic and symptomatic factors that death anxiety, especially of the existential variety, arises not only from anxiety over physical death but also arises from some implicit awareness of the death of the soul, of living too much according to mortalizing passion, of living too much in what the ancients understood to be vice.

Otherwise put, existential death anxiety is a syndrome produced not only by anxiety over physical death but also resonates with and, in the end, includes a second anxiety, easily missed if one insists that death anxiety is only about the cessation of life. This second anxiety concerns the "death of the soul," born of living too much according to mortalizing and uncultivated instinctual and passional life and insufficiently responsive to the *nous* or the Self. If the ancients are correct on this point, it buttresses Jung's belief that death has a meaning beyond being the mere cessation of life: Evidently, intrinsic to the teleological life process is the call to cultivate one's instinctual life in attunement to one's responsiveness to the divine or the *nous* or the Self—whatever form one's understanding of the divine might be—and any substantive and habitual turning of that responsiveness away from that proper orientation brings with it anxiety over death, not only the death of the body but also the death of the soul.

Toward a Clinical Ethics

I have suggested that these points are relevant to clinical ethics, and one may be wondering why I think so. But if we follow the analysis of the ancient philosophers to its logical conclusion, it becomes clear that it has everything to do with ethics. But first, we may need to adjust our understanding of ethics.

In our time, especially in professional settings, discussions in "ethics" usually refer to laws and rules pertaining to the treatment of others, what we might term an "extraverted" ethics, since it focuses on others and on the outer world. For the ancient philosophers, there certainly is such an extraverted ethics, but it is generally a function of what we might correspondingly call an "introverted" ethics, an ethics described in terms of the health and illness of the psyche or soul. As we saw, for Cicero as well as for others among the ancient philosophers, the psyche itself could be healthy or ill, and its fundamental illness arises from a rejection or renunciation or misuse of the noetic function of the mind and immersion in mortalizing passion, potentially to the point that one could, metaphorically, "kill the soul."

This analysis, of course, has the character of a diagnosis, highlighting what occurs when one loses the balance of consciousness through unresponsiveness or poor responsiveness to the *nous* or the Self. It is with the attempted solution to this problem that we find the ethical component which potentially has relevance to mental health professionals. For if the psyche, by nature, is meant to live a tensional existence, that fact entails that one articulate a way of making oneself habitually responsive to the *nous* or to the Self while simultaneously developing habits that cultivate the lower psyche and body, such that they can be impacted by the responsive experiences to the divine. Tensions are, by definition, less than stable. Consequently, developing certain kinds of "habit" as a stabilizing element is arguably the key point here. Occasional bouts of entering into "mortalizing passion," let's say an excessive celebration after a Superbowl victory, does not by itself constitute anything like the death of the soul, as already Plato's *Symposium* illustrates. Rather, the issue concerns one's *habitual orientation*: To what extent is one generally and habitually responsive to the *nous* or the Self or habitually mired in mortalizing passions, to the point that one partakes of the "nothingness" of mortality more than the immortality born of responsiveness to the divine?

The nature of habit is broached to some extent in Jungian literature, but primarily in terms of typology, for example whether one is introverted or extraverted, or for example a thinker or feeler, suggesting here that the issue of habit pertains solely to questions about the modes of adaptation (Jung, 1923a, 1923b; White, 2023). The philosophers, in contrast, were concerned with habit not primarily in terms of the dominant form of adaptation, but rather in terms of whether one cultivated the soul, in particular, cultivated desires, so that one's desires in general led one to a life formed by the *nous* and habituated the instincts and animal nature in a way at least coherent and hopefully expressive of a positive life narrative. This is less about orientations of adaptation than developing habits conducive to whatever appear to be the better aspirations of the person.

The traditional language for this sort of habit is *virtue*. In our time, the concept of virtue has been somewhat subverted—when it is mentioned at all—as, for example, in the contemporary notion of "virtue signaling." Whatever the value of that latter notion in its own context, it links virtue with moralism, dogmatism, and external control, something quite inimical to the original understanding of virtue. The ancient concept of virtue was not moralistic at all because it was not about any external constraining of behavior; it was, rather, about cultivating desires in such a way that, over time, one actually *wanted* to do what was best and right and in one's own best interests. Just as the term "cultivation" suggests, one is not trying to repress desires, but rather orient and habituate them toward positive ends, and do so oneself and from one's own responsiveness to the divine or the Self, not by external constraint (MacIntyre, 2022). The assumption here, which I believe can be verified by each of us phenomenologically, is that instinctual desires, as a rule, tend to be indiscriminate in their ends and are rarely good guides as to how best to fulfill themselves in a way consistent with one's best life narrative. The same desire for food, drink, sex, or sleep, for example, sometimes leads to ends conducive to one's life goals and other times leads one away from them. Thus, something else must, as it were, be added to instinctual impulses and desires to render them more useful to our proper life goals.

This additional something is virtue. Virtue, then, is a developed habit orienting desires, instincts, and impulses in such a way that they serve our life projects, presumably in part determined by our responsiveness to the Self (Aristotle, 1982; Voegelin, 2000). I hope it is clear already at this point that virtue is not repressive because it does not seek to limit desires per se, but order and channel desires toward some vision of what counts as good. Indeed, a virtuous person potentially feels desire more intensely than the non-virtuous because the narrower channel, so to speak, intensifies the momentum. Virtues are neither puritanical nor prudish, because they assume that desires are basically good but are generally in need of cultivation and habit to make them such they typically work in the direction of a positive and determinate end (MacIntyre, 2022).

I mentioned earlier that the philosophers understood the psyche to live in tensions, one of which was that between existence toward the immortal *nous* and the gravitational pull of the animal in us toward mortalizing passion. According to Aristotle's version of virtue, however, there is a second tension, one which also helps define virtues. We might call it a "horizontal tension" in contrast to the "vertical tension" mentioned already. Virtues, Aristotle says, are a mean between extremes—what more popularly and once upon a time was called "the golden mean." For example, Aristotle says courage—a virtue—is a mean between two extremes which are vices, one of excess, which he terms rashness, and one of deficiency, which is cowardice. Each of the vices is, of course, infected with mortalizing passion, because they lack the balance of consciousness and, above all, the prudence associated with genuine courage and are ultimately born of mortalizing passion. So we notice according to Aristotle's picture that, once again, a kind of "middle way" (or In-Between), is where one finds the healthy place for the soul (Aristotle, 1982; Voegelin, 2000).

Consequently, a desire counts as virtuous when one develops it habitually in a way (1) consistent with the positive realization of human nature (i.e., in response to the pulling from the *nous*/Self) (Voegelin, 1995), (2) conducive to one's positive life narrative (e.g., concrete relationships, professional requirements, etc.) (MacIntyre, 2022), and (3) representative of a conscious balance of tensions (Voegelin, 1995). Typically, virtues are developed through a hit-and-miss process, a fact important not only for understanding the nature of virtue but also for, again, recognizing why a virtue ethics isn't or at least needn't be moralistic. The very development of virtue respects process: It is not like a legalistic approach to ethics whereby one has either followed the law or failed. Rather one can have more or less virtue, and it is assumed at the outset that, like anything having the quality of a habit, it requires a hit-and-miss process and ongoing development.

Though this is an "introverted" ethics, because it focuses on internal development of attitudes, instincts, and so forth from within, it should be clear that it also has "extraverted" effects because, after all, if I develop, say, a virtue like justice, though it does have to do with my inner attitudes, it also affects all my relationships: The more I develop the balance of consciousness associated with the virtue of justice, the more I will tend to act justly when occasions arise. One of the purposes of the virtuous habit, in fact, is to render positive actions more probable. But notice, the emphasis on internal cultivation and change is nonetheless important. For example, a generally unjust person can, at times, perform a just act, but one of the consequences of becoming a just person is that one *typically* performs just acts by having habituated one's instincts and desires toward balance and justice.

Perhaps that is enough for the general theory. How does this help with clinical ethics? It focuses our attention, first and foremost, not on our patient, but on the sort of person we ourselves are in our dealings with our patients. The law-based or rule-based approach that I have termed an "extraverted" ethics is a perfectly good guide for how to act—or actually, more frequently, about how *not* to act, since most rules are about constricting negative actions, not encouraging positive actions. But were we, first and foremost, to understand our clinical ethics in terms of virtue, our first work as clinicians would be about cultivating habitual and positive attitudes so that the latter are always already there, lying in wait, as it were, for occasions when they could be exercised. If a person chooses to be a just person by habit in the first place, that person will not find a rule about being just to clients to be in any way constricting. Reasonable ethical rules are experienced as constricting only when one has *not* developed the appropriate habitual attitude or virtue in the first place (MacIntyre, 2022).

Much of what I have said, though I have couched it in philosophical terms, is already present in the classical psychoanalytic tradition, though it has not been conceived of from an ethical standpoint. Let's take as an example the classical psychoanalytic approach to managing affect. From the very roots of psychoanalysis, the problem of how to relate to affect has been a trope, the very notion of repression referring first and foremost to affect. Now to summarize one classical approach to affect, we can say there are three basic options in relation to affect: repression, whereby one virtually cuts off conscious contact with affect; "acting out," as when one vents or otherwise lives out an affective disturbance, usually thereby depositing one's affect on others; or, third, a middle way, which consists of containing the affect consciously and thus not repressing it, but also not acting it out, because it is contained (Goodheart, 1980; Langs, 1978). And in and through that containment, one can begin to understand, work with, and learn from the affect how best to manage it and what it might mean psychologically. Notice how well the Aristotelian analysis might fit here: (1) If repressed, the affect cannot come into the sphere of being influenced by the *nous* or by the Self due to its unconsciousness and is thus merely "mortalizing" affect. On the other hand, if it is left to itself and merely acted out, its energy and life is frittered away, and again there is no way to consciously link it to the Self. But if it is contained without repressing and experienced without being acted out, it is possible for the affect to come under the influence of the Self, the "immortalizing" principle.

Similar examples could be given, ranging over basic clinical attitudes such as empathy or the use of interventions like interpretation, of which the typical descriptions in psychoanalytic literature suggest the classical virtue of *phronesis* or prudence. In fact, a more detailed analysis would find that the logic of the virtuous "middle way" is essential to psychological health, especially in the Jungian tradition, and that the attainment of that middle way virtually always functions in a way similar to Aristotle's analysis, but with this difference: More often than not, psychoanalytic traditions do not have a robust theory of habit and how to develop it positively, at least in the ethical sense of habit, something which is quite central to the ancient picture of virtue.

If this understanding of virtue is on target, part of our work as analysts concerns not only our personal psychological work, something Jung always emphasized, but potentially also our personal *ethical* work, understanding by "ethics" the cultivation of instinctual and passional life in a way that is expressive of and conducive to our responsiveness to the Self, including the work of developing virtue. Without this work, it would seem, we will tend to find ourselves too caught up in the problems of existential death anxiety and less able to help our patients when they find that they are caught up in it too.

Conclusion

Let me conclude by tying up especially several clinical loose ends. If the analysis I have offered is basically correct, we can accept Langs' analysis of death anxiety and its articulation of symptom formations. Yet, at least from a broadly Western and certainly from a Jungian perspective, we need to modify it in certain directions, by giving it a larger context.

First, though Langs' understanding of death anxiety offers important insights into its nature and treatment, his general assumptions, which tend to be both materialist and atheist, may exclude certain clinically important phenomena from the outset. For if it is the case that death anxiety is not only about the death of the body but also what we termed "the death of the soul," these symptom formations require treatment of both conditions, not only of the symptoms themselves but also of the mortalizing passion which underlies them. Furthermore, I might even suggest that once the death of the soul is recognized as an actual phenomenon, it may indicate that Jung is correct in thinking that death is the proper end of the life process and also that intrinsic to that goal is the positive cultivation of the passions described as virtue.

Consequently, when death anxiety and its symptoms are habitual in a patient, it is probably not enough to try to alleviate the symptoms through "secured frame" therapy, as Langs thought, least of all during a pandemic when existential death anxiety is running amok and given that secured frame of therapy itself exacerbates the death anxiety. Rather, as a therapist, one should *also* be looking for where there appears to be an excess of mortalizing passion, that is, a habitual affective, instinctive, or desire-based psychic impulse which appears either disconnected from a conscious relationship to the Self and/or inconsistent with the patient's ultimate and positive life narrative, which is also acting up, due to the death anxiety. Indications of death anxiety as well as Cicero's list of syndromes would be, for example, fair game clinically.

Third, we might postulate the idea that, if one accepts that death anxiety is not only about the death of the body but also about the death of the soul, we might find a way out of the analytic conundrum Langs highlights, namely that secured frame therapy is the only way to heal death anxiety but also itself produces death anxiety. Once we recognize the possibility that death anxiety is not only about physical death but also about areas of uncultivated instinctual life which demand cultivation, many of which might be associated with the specific symptoms both Langs and Cicero develop, it may require a clinical focus on the uncultivated instincts and ordering them through responsiveness to the Self—more or less a definition of individuation and a concept lacking in Langs' theories (White, 2023). This, in turn, will result in the diminishment of the paradox of secured frame therapy.[4]

Fourth, if we take for granted—as I do—that, as Harold Searles put it, patients are always trying unconsciously to make us the therapist they need, we clinicians should assume that—when we run into death anxiety—there is an ethical call being issued to us. If we find we ourselves are resonating with the patient's death anxiety in ways that seem strange or excessive, as I noted about my own experiences above, chances are there are places of mortalizing passion *in us* that are in need of being brought to consciousness and cultivation, that need to be consciously related to the

Self and to our better life narrative. As Jung frequently suggested, we can only bring our patients so far down this road if we have not already walked it ourselves.

The age of pandemic is not only an age of death anxiety but potentially an invitation to develop virtue by making the uncultivated passions like those articulated by Cicero conscious and developing a habitual redirection of those passions by conscious connection to the Self. We clinicians must stand, if not comfortably, at least consciously, in between life and death and recognize where the death of the soul may be manifesting, in us and in our patients, amidst the anxiety over bodily death. If we can manage to do that, we may find that death may no longer seem merely like the cessation of life, but rather more like the meaningful end and fulfillment of life that Jung and the ancient philosophers suggest it is.

Notes

1 Though the "soul murder" of Schreber can sound similar, it is a different phenomenon altogether from what the philosophers called the "death of the soul."
2 At the time of his own death, Langs was working on a psychoanalytic study of the US Presidents, which purported to show how death-related traumas and death denial loom large in each of their lives and illustrating how each of them both "make it to the top," but do so at the cost of their psychological health and the wellbeing of others.
3 The crucial issue is whether they are attempts at an equivalent symbolization of the same phenomenon or not, not whether they are textually defined in precisely the same way or with quite the same function within their differing systems of thought.
4 A further point that I only add in passing is that certain aspects of American life exude death anxiety and death denial, mostly associated with the materialism of consumer capitalism and the close connection between social status and the ownership of capital, which more or less entail a number of the attitudes which Cicero isolated as "diseases of the soul." A fuller analysis of this issue can be found in (White, 2022).

References

Aristotle. (1982). *The Nicomachean ethics* (H. Rackham, Trans.). Harvard University Press.

Becker, E. (2020). *The denial of death*. Souvenir Press.

Cicero, M. T. (2018). *Cicero 18: Tusculan disputations* (J. E. King, Trans.). Harvard University Press.

Goodheart, W. (1980). Theory of analytic interaction. *San Francisco Library Jung Institute Journal, 1*, 2–39.

Heidegger, M. (2010). *Being and time* (J. Stambaugh, Trans.). State University of New York Press.

Jung, C. G. (1923a). Psychological types. In R. F. C. Hull (Trans.), *Psychological types* (Vol. CW 6, pp. 510–523). Princeton University Press.

Jung, C. G. (1923b). *Psychological types* (R. F. C. Hull, Trans., Vol. CW 6). Princeton University Press.

Jung, C. G. (1931). The stages of life. In R. F. C. Hull (Trans.), *The structure and dynamics of the psyche* (Vol. CW 8, pp. 387–403). Princeton University Press.

Jung, C. G. (1934). Soul and death. In R. F. C. Hull (Trans.), *The structure and dynamics of the psyche* (Vol. CW 8, pp. 404–415). Princeton University Press.

Jung, C. G. (1969). The transcendent function. In R. F. C. Hull (Trans.), *The structure and dynamics of the psyche* (Vol. CW 8, pp. 67–91). Princeton University Press.

Langs, R. (1978). *The listening process*. Jason Aronson.

Langs, R. (2004a). Death anxiety and the emotion-processing mind. *Psychoanalytic Psychology, 21*(1), 31–53.

Langs, R. (2004b). *Fundamentals of adaptive psychotherapy and counseling*. Palgrave Macmillan.

Langs, R. (2005). The challenge of the strong adaptive approach. *Psychoanalytic Psychology, 22*(1), 49–68.

Langs, R. (2010). *Freud on a precipice: How Freud's fate pushed psychoanalysis over the edge*. Jason Aronson.

MacIntyre, A. (2022). *After virtue: A study in moral theory*. University of Notre Dame Press.

Voegelin, E. (1995). Reason: The classic experience. In G. Niemeyer (Ed.), *Anamnesis*. University of Missouri Press.

Voegelin, E. (2000). *Plato and Aristotle* (P. G. Caringella, Ed.). University of Missouri Press.

White, J. (2019). Jung, the numinous and the philosophers: On immanence and transcendence in religious experience. In J. Mills (Ed.), *Jung and philosophy* (pp. 186–203). Routledge.

White, J. (2022). Colonizing the American psyche: Virtue and the problem of consumer capitalism. In J. Mills & D. Burston (Eds.), *Critical theory and psychoanalysis: From the Frankfurt school to contemporary critique* (pp. 211–230). Routledge.

White, J. (2023). *Adaptation and psychotherapy: Langs and analytical psychology*. Rowman & Littlefield.

Index

ecopsychology 134–135, 150
Edinger, Edward 15, 23, 26, 27, 28, 54, 127
ego-Nature axis 23, 25, 26
ego-Self axis 10, 23, 26
Ellenberger, Henri F. 161
EMDR (eye movement desensitization and
    reprocessing) 25
Émile (Rousseau) 80
Enough (McKibben) 9
environmental contamination 16–17; risk
    assessment 20
environmental damage from animal
    agriculture 90–91
environmental trauma 24–25
ethics, clinical 164–169
existential death anxiety 155–156, 158,
    163–164

factory farming 84–96
Fairbairn, Ronald 33
fairy tales 147–148
fate/Fates 62–63
Fellows, Andrew 27
fire issues, environmental 17–18
Floyd, George 32, 45, 46–47
Foer, Jonathan Safran 77, 92, 94–95
food-borne disease 88
food chain 88; *see also* animal
    (non-human) abuse
Frazier, Darnella 45, 49
Freud, Sigmund: on death 95; on feminine
    sexuality 67; on violence 79–80
Fuentes, Carlos 104, 105–106, 112

Gaia hypothesis 10
Galeano, Eduardo 100
Gandhi, Mahatma 35–36, 39
gardens 142–143
Giedion, Siegfried 94
Girard, Rene 80
Golden, Carl 150
Graves, Robert 129
Great Lakes region 141–142
Great Mother archetype 138
Grimm Brothers fairy tales 147–148
gun culture in the U.S.: Ares archetype
    124, 125–127; Ares energy as "inner
    gun" 127, 131; case studies 128–131;
    gun complex 122–125; gun debate,
    gridlock of 122–124; and psychanalysis
    127–128; symbolism of guns
    117–122, 132

Guntrip, Harry 71
Gustafson, Fred 62, 139, 143

Hadas, Pamela 65
Hansen, James 149–150
Harding, Esther 68
Harris, Eric 117
heavy metals 14
Heidegger, Martin 162
Hill, John 105
Hill, Julia Butterfly 9
Hillman, James 101, 114, 119, 123, 124,
    135; models for consciousness/psyche
    136, 141
Holliday, Billie 111
hope 49–50, 53
Human Aggression (Storr) 127
Human Destructiveness (Storr) 127
Hunter of Good Heart image 82–83, 95–96

I Ching 140, 145
Idea of the Holy (Otto) 126–127
imaginal view of life 100–101, 114, 143
I-Nature relationships 10, 11, 15–16
In-Between, soul as 160, 161, 162
indigenous peoples: and imaginal view of
    life 100–101; and interconnectedness
    135; and Jungian ecological models
    138–139; papal bull on humanity of
    100; under Spanish conquest 100–101;
    sweat lodge ceremonies 150; vision
    quests 138–139
individuation 26, 39; as creative process
    126, 132
Inslee, Jay 52
interconnectedness 135, 151
intersection, symbolism of 15, 52–53, 105
Irigaray, Luce 72
"Iron Hans" fairy tale 148
Iron John (Bly) 148
I-Thou/I-Other relationships 10

Jacobi, Jolanda 15, 26, 28
jihad 36–37
Jung, Carl Gustav: on analytic third
    13; archetypal perspective on
    ecopsychology 134; BBC interview
    (1959) 149–150; *Black Books* 61; on
    Cartesian-Christian attitudes 106–107;
    collective psyche and culture 61–63;
    concept of Self 27; on conviction in
    psychology 11; on creative instinct